D0428657

IN THE ABSENCE OF GOD

ALSO BY SAM KEEN

Sightings

Faces of the Enemy

Learning to Fly

To Love and Be Loved

Hymns to an Unknown God

Inward Bound

Fire in the Belly

Your Mythic Journey

The Passionate Life

Beginnings Without End

To a Dancing God

Apology for Wonder

Gabriel Marcel

IN THE
ABSENCE
OF
GOD

*Dwelling in the
Presence of
the Sacred*

SAM KEEN

HARMONY BOOKS • New York

Library of Congress Cataloging-in-Publication Data
Keen, Sam.
In the absence of God / Sam Keen. — 1st ed.
p. cm.
1. Spirituality. 2. Spiritual life. 3. Religion. I. Title.
BL624.K4424 2010
204—dc22
2009030672

ISBN 978-0-307-46229-9

Printed in the United States of America

Design by Helene Berinsky

10 9 8 7 6 5 4 3 2 1

First Edition

CONTENTS

IN THE ABSENCE OF GOD

The God-Shaped Vacuum

There is a God-shaped vacuum in the heart of every man which cannot be filled by any created thing.

—BLAISE PASCAL

Digging beneath my immediate mind, which distracts itself with pizza, paper clips, and the rising and falling of the Dow, I uncover ruins of old dwellings, a house, a temple, and a town square once occupied, believed in, faithfully tended.

I stumble, unstable on shifting ground. My mind wanders through layers of rubble, discarded beliefs, outworn creeds, broken hopes, shattered illusions, bones of failed heroes and false saviors.

Socrates, that old trickster, taught me a way of thinking, dialectic and dialogue, an endless approach. But I never arrived at the promised vision of the good, the beautiful, and the true.

I believed in the Lord Jesus Christ, with as much heart, mind, and soul as I could manage, but he failed to saved me from death's dominion and the fear of nothingness.

I trusted Freud to lead me down into an underworld (neither he nor I conquered) from which I returned wounded, with little redemptive wisdom other than a sermon on coping and the virtues of love and work.

Marx, in whom I never believed, taught me better than he knew the danger of all utopias and left me with the bitter truth that I and all the bourgeoisie are moved more by desire for power and profit than by love of justice.

Tiring of pure reason, I dreamed of the dark kingdom of Dionysus, an orgy of the senses to wash away the pale abstractions of the mind. In time I learned what Apollo knows: Order may be sweet, and discipline a path to delight.

A skilled archeologist might map more layers, passions, persons, and places that I thought might save me— from what I am not certain—and give me peace at last.

Should I mourn and build again? Clear away the debris, smooth out the ground, prepare a solid foundation for a new edifice to house my spirit?

Wherever I stand, tectonic plates rumble. I am earthquake-prone. Not a good insurance risk.

I think it is better to dwell in the desert under open skies, look for hidden oases, make a hearth, light a fire, cherish sunrise, noonday, moonset, a flight of Canada geese, an ant empire being built an arm's length away, the comfort of touch, the language of glances, smiles, laughter, tears—sacred moments.

Be thankful for the myriad hints of a G-d present in absence, in the longing without end. Amen.

• • •

We who have been unsatisfied by any traditional religion have spent our lives in quest of a rose, but the closest we ever get is entering a room still redolent with the scent of a rose that was removed before we arrived. We cannot easily locate God in the house of our longing, yet we remain haunted; God's missing presence echoes throughout the empty rooms. In the void we hear faint hymns of an ancient faith for which we no longer have room among the endless quarks, waves, and subatomic particles identified by science. We exist in a God-shaped vacuum. That which is no longer present (but is not completely absent) gives shape to our aspirations and longings.

Although longing seems to be perennial, the historical tide of faith ebbs and flows. Currently in the industrialized nations it seems to have receded, depositing its driftwood of nihilism and violence on the shore, leaving us devoid of a vision of the sacred that we need in order to create a hopeful society. We suffer from a spiritual autoimmune disease. Lacking antibodies of faith to keep us from despair, we attack ourselves.

We are trapped in a life in which little attention is paid to the encompassing mystery of Being traditionally known by the Ten Thousand Names of God. Many of us feel the loss of this absent God, and we feel outrage. You can hear it in the voices of the new atheologians who condemn the violence of religious fundamentalism but are angry that a God in whom they do not believe does not prevent holocausts or provide verifiable evidence of His existence. It is painful to be aware of what is missing, but the experience of longing should not be denied, covered up, or tranquilized. It is precisely from this point that we may start on a path toward renewal.

Our experience of absence rests firmly upon an ancient memory of presence. The premise and promise of this book is that if we have the courage to wait patiently on the border between agnosticism and faith, forsaking the false certainties promised by the God of traditional religion (a God whose nature and name true believers presume to know), we may find ourselves encompassed by the G-d of the mystics, the ultimate reality that energizes all beings but can only be named in the gossamer language of myth and metaphor and poetry. (Note: Throughout, I will continue to use "God" and "G-d" to differentiate traditional from mystical religion.) As we will find, only by rediscovering the elementary emotions that accompany the experience of the sacred—wonder, awe, gratitude, anxiety, joy, grief, reverence, empowerment, vocation, compassion, outrage, hope, humility, trust—may we once again find ourselves in the presence of an unknowable but all-present G-d.

> Hold a chambered shell to your ear and you will hear the undulating surge and sigh of the primal sea.
>
> —SANDOR MCNAB

I

Idolatrous Gods and Profane Ideologies

Turning and turning in the widening gyre
The falcon cannot hear the falconer;
Things fall apart; the center cannot hold;
Mere anarchy is loosed upon the world,
The blood-dimmed tide is loosed, and everywhere
The ceremony of innocence is drowned;
The best lack all conviction, while the worst
Are full of passionate intensity.

—W. B. YEATS

Much of the contemporary world is torn between violent gods and soulless economics, dogmatic religion and a profane void. The honorable name of an ancient God is being used to sanctify war and the demonic designs of tribes, nations, and empires. Technical intelligence threatens the blessed earth. The sacred is eclipsed, our spiritscape desecrated. It is a confusing time to think about religion.

The closing decades of the twentieth century were marked by optimistic predictions that we were on the road to social, economic, and technological progress. We thought that after an estimated one hundred million deaths from state-and-church-sponsored violence we had seen through the utopias promised by conventional religion and secular ideology. But we were wrong.

Instead we are experiencing a resurgence of militant fundamentalism, holy war, and theocracy. Already in this new millennium, hot-blooded religious fanatics of all persuasions have butchered millions of innocents. The ancient demigods of tribes and empires, the landlord deities, and the political idols have returned. Once again we hear the demonic claim that the time has come to rise up and smite the evil ones—Hutus, Serbs, Americans, Arabs, Jews, Muslims, and Christians. How quickly we have forgotten that talk of God and country, of infidels and axes of evil, is just politicized idolatry to justify murdering the Other.

Instead of confronting our global problems—poverty, injustice, hunger, environmental degradation, and the proliferation of weapons of mass destruction and small arms—our imaginations have been seized by something akin to our love of Disneyland. Both religious institutions and secular governments have chosen to hide their heads in the sand and promote fantasies of apocalyptic and utopian futures.

Untold millions of Christians, Jews, and Christian Zionists imagine that spiritual renewal will arrive in the form of the apocalypse that will take place when the Jews have all returned to Israel. More than half of all Americans believe that the end-of-times events predicted in the book of Revelation will come to pass. Of those who believe Armageddon is just around the corner, 47 percent believe the Antichrist is on earth now, and 45 percent believe that Jesus will return during their lifetime. For these believers the future is clear. With the Antichrist in power, life on earth will be a living hell for those who remain, but just in the nick of time Jesus will come again, and gather his born-again children in a rapture. The graves of the saved will open, family members will be snatched up from the dinner table, pilots plucked from their planes, and lovers interrupted midcourse. After a terrible war in which most people on earth will die, Christ will come for a third time and rule over the earth for one thousand years, ushering in a golden era of universal peace. Following Christ's millennial reign, history will end, followed by a new heaven and a new earth.

The eschatology of Muslims is only slightly less dramatic. It centers on the appearance of the Mahdi, a messianic figure whom Shia Muslims identify as the hidden imam, who will put an end to the suffering of Muslims and bring justice to the world. Surprisingly, Jesus makes a cameo appearance in the Islamic version of the end-time. According to the Qur'an, Jesus will return and destroy the Antichrist. Then the Mahdi will complete the spread of Islam and reestablish the Caliphate. The armed radical wing of Islam expects, with or without the help of the Mahdi, to defeat the godless West and establish a global Islamic order.

Watching the bloody acts of violence committed in the name of religion, reasonable people will naturally wonder why they should have anything to do with it. Regrettably, the secular ideologies of our time that compete with religion for our hearts and minds have created their own fantastical vision of the end-time. For unredeemed secular optimists the myth of progress continues to forecast a bright, if not utopian, future. The new prime mover that will lead us into the global empire of milk and honey is not God but a global conglomerate. The promised alabaster city undimmed by human tears morphs into the Mall of America.

Americans are profoundly schizophrenic, split between expecting Jesus to return and hoping for the coming triumph of liberal democracy. In this land of TV evangelists and Wal-Mart, fundamentalism and modernity cohabit more amiably than Democrats and Republicans. And the best part of the triumphant future promised by the evangelists of progress is that it is already here! In *The End of*

History and the Last Man, Francis Fukuyama argues that liberal democracy is the final form of government, the pinnacle of humanity's ideological evolution. In the last century it has conquered all its rivals—monarchy, fascism, and communism—proof positive that this is the secular utopia toward which all human life has been struggling. We are the last ones, the expected ones, the culmination of history's dialectic. Fukuyama puts it this way: "If we looked beyond liberal democracy and markets, there was nothing else toward which we could expect to evolve because they are the only political system that satisfies individuals' desire for recognition and dignity. Hence the end of history."

In spite of recent setbacks on the road to utopia, the vast majority of Americans still retain a dogged belief in American exceptionalism and the eventual return of an economy that will allow us to enjoy unrestrained consumption and military dominance sufficient to remain the world's only superpower. We may be down at the moment, but we'll bounce back up before long. The U.S. presidential election of 2008 was won with bywords that captured the perennial optimism of the American spirit. Change! Hope! Yes we can!

But this knee-jerk optimism ignores a multitude of problems. (A multitude of sins?) We live by the grace of an unacknowledged inheritance from a rich godfather. The "civil" in our civilization was created by generations whose religious institutions taught them that the golden rule and the inalienable rights of citizens were ordained by God. Civic religion inculcated the virtues of care for our neighbor and sacrifice for the common good. But our inheritance is running out.

It is doubtful that the imperatives springing from modern secularism can create a civil community. How can a consumer economy justify sacrifice, generosity, and the commitment of time and energy to nurture the young? In a culture that worships efficiency, speed, profit, and consumption, where do we get the mandate to love one another, to feel compassion toward those who are sick, unemployed, homeless, or old (i.e., "useless")? I can't help wondering if the idea of a secular civilization is an oxymoron, a failed dream of the Enlightenment.

Without some vision of the sacred, what will be the source of compassion, sacrifice, and mutual care, without which there can be no commonwealth? How will we discover values that transcend the selfish interests of the ego, the family, the tribe, the corporation, and the nation? How will we learn compassion for a stranger? Where will we get that sense of reverence for life that is the cornerstone of the desire to preserve our environment? Where shall we look for hope?

Can we reasonably hope that multinational corporations will get a heart, like the Tin Man in *The Wizard of Oz,* and become more concerned for the common good than for the bottom line? Can we reasonably hope that politicians and journalists, like the Scarecrow, will get a brain and present complex issues to the public rather than invent scapegoats and enemies? Can we reasonably hope that the military establishment, like the Cowardly Lion, will stop hiding behind women and children, reject the policy of acceptable collateral damage, and find the courage to become a peacemaker? Can we reasonably hope that technophiles will develop the social conscience to devote themselves only to creative innovations—not to inventing more and better weapons of mass destruction? Can we reasonably hope that consumers will learn the meaning of *enough,* and hold off on buying luxuries until everyone has necessities? Can we reasonably hope that the complacent majority of good Christians, good Jews, good Muslims, and good Hindus will demand that their leaders stop sanctifying the violence of empire and jihad in order to create a compassionate commonwealth of all sentient beings?

Absent these slim hopes, Dorothy will never find her way back home to Kansas. Failing our rediscovery of the virtues of reverence and respect, our future on this planet looks dark and brutish—and very short indeed. In a brilliant and disturbing article, "The Slow Apocalypse: A Gradualistic Theory of the World's Demise," Andrew McMurry argues that the four horsemen of the modern apocalypse—arms proliferation, environmental degradation, the crisis of meaning, and the malignant global economy—are already riding roughshod over the earth. The mushroom cloud is already rising above us, and our leading nations lack the collective will to do anything about our precarious situation. He concludes that our hyper-complex civilization may be nothing more than an evolutionary blind alley.

But before we despair over this bleak scenario we should ask if there is a hopeful alternative to the relentless onslaught of fundamentalism and nihilistic secularism. Is there a way out of limbo for those of us who are unable to believe in the miracles, mystery, and authority offered by institutional religion yet are unable to thrive in the spiritual poverty of our economic ideology?

I suggest that there is, if we know where to look.

Surprisingly, the renewal we seek is most likely to come from a new understanding of what lies at the heart of religion. The vision we require is not missing, only forgotten. It sleeps in the taproot from which religion originally grew—the kaleidoscopic richness of our experience of the sacred. We have been looking in all the wrong places.

The word *religion* covers a vast and vague territory. Under the same umbrella it includes gentle Quakers and ruthless jihadists, sedate Episcopalians and shouting tent evangelists, rock-and-roll mega-churches and solitary monks. Any analysis of religion must acknowledge that it includes both the best and the worst of human endeavor. In these pages I will attempt to peel away the shell of the many formal expressions of religion and get to the meat, the living heart of the matter: the experience that all authentically religious persons share of living within a world that is sacred.

Each of the great world religions—Buddhism, Hinduism, Judaism, Christianity, and Islam—is a braid woven from four strands: an originating experience, a mythic narrative, a theology, and an institution. In the beginning a solitary man—Buddha, Moses, Jesus, Muhammad—had a numinous encounter that filled him with a sense of power and purpose—a voice coming from a burning bush or from the depths of the soul. Following this life-changing experience, these great pathfinders shared their insights with a few men and women who became disciples and formed the master's story into a coherent narrative.

In time, the narrative gave rise to scriptures, creeds, and theologies. Gradually, temples, churches, mosques, and synagogues encapsulated the primal experience of the sacred in formal rites, rituals, and narratives, each claiming to be the definitive revelation of the transcendent God. As Emerson put it, in the first generation, the men were golden and the goblets were wooden; in the second generation, the goblets were golden and the men were wooden. To the degree that any religion focuses the attention and devotion of believers on the official narrative, theology, and liturgical practices of the institution, it obscures the primal or elementary experience of the sacred that is our common birthright.

Broadly speaking, institutional religions come in three varieties—conservative, reactionary, and progressive. The world over, conservatives, who draw quiet strength and comfort from the faith of their fathers, make up the majority of believers. They feel little need to jettison the narrative within which they are at home. To varying degrees the experience of the sacred remains alive and well within the protective walls of conservative synagogues, churches, mosques, and temples. The danger of conservatism is that it tends to defend the status quo. It encourages uncritical allegiance to the tradition and discourages critical investigation of the scriptures and the politics of the establishment. Under pressure it becomes reactionary.

Reactionaries and fundamentalists stake their claims to The Truth based on scripture taken out of context. They tolerate no questioning the authority of their interpretations or their clerical leaders. Since they are convinced they possess the one true religion, they often advocate the creation of a theocracy that will enforce the divinely revealed laws—a global Islamic order, Jewish state, or Christian republic. In pursuit of their vision of God they render violence sacred and wage holy wars. They are noticeably lacking in imagination, sense of humor, and the capacity for self-criticism.

Progressives cherish their tradition's symbols, narratives, myths, and doctrines but do not take them literally. Consequently, they respect other traditions and cultivate interfaith dialogue. They have been the leaders in promoting historical and critical approaches to scripture, translating the language of ancient myth into modern equivalents and locating the essence of religion in the individual's spiritual quest, in the experience of community, and in the struggle for social justice.

It is from the progressive tradition, from the recovery of the personal encounter with the sacred in ordinary life, and from the change in the locus of religious authority, that we may expect renewal to come.

Hidden in the word *authority* is both the diagnosis and cure for the disease that authoritarian religions and political systems inflict on unquestioning believers. An authority is any person or institution that claims to be the *author* of the story, myth, narrative, and values by which we should live. The revitalization of religion can only happen when individuals reclaim the authority of their own experience of the sacred and create narratives allowing them to share this experience with other members of their communities.

Religion is a powerful source of either despair or hope, depending on whether it continues to create self-serving institutions or struggles to bring reverence and compassion back into the center of our individual and communal lives. It maintains its vitality and ability to transform culture only when it points beyond church, nation, and marketplace to stand as a witness to the universal sacred dimension of all life.

Fortunately, a renewal of the vision of the sacred does not depend solely on people or institutions that are formally religious. Recent brain research has confirmed what religious mystics have always known. Something very like an instinct for the sacred is triggered by our awareness of the limitless creativity of the cosmos, of the fragility of the human condition, and of our absolute dependence on a source of life that is beyond our control. Because of the essential limits of our knowledge, power, and time we inevitably seek to transcend our finitude.

In a 2008 article in the *New York Times* titled "The Neural Buddhists," David Brooks wrote, "People are equipped to experience the sacred, to have moments of elevated experience when they transcend boundaries and overflow with love. . . . God can best be conceived as the nature one experiences at those moments, the unknowable total of all there is." In light of the growing awareness that the human mind is calibrated to experience the sacred, Brooks concludes that the ground of the debate about religion has shifted. "The real challenge is going to come from people who feel the existence of the sacred, but who think that particular religions are just cultural artifacts built on top of universal human traits."

No one can predict what might happen should there be a renewal of the sense of the sacred in conventional religious institutions, or what new myths, metaphors, parables, rituals, and disciplines might infuse the twenty-first century with hope. But we can begin to collect the fragments of the whole-hearted religion that all peoples could share equally.

Why fragments? We are in an era in which our old myths, paradigms, and institutions are being overwhelmed. The barbarians have breached the gates. We can all recite the laundry list of global problems and troubling contradictions we face. But new organizing myths are not simply invented. They emerge gradually, piece by piece, when cultures face challenges that force them to change—or die.

This book focuses on the perennial experience of the sacred that has long been ignored, shrouded, and repressed by profane culture but is once again coming to light. The recovery of this experiential heart of living religion is essential if we are to allow our diverse commonwealth of living beings to dwell in harmony in the twenty-first century.

In the chapters that follow, I will attempt to spell out

what it means to experience the world as a sacred place. My hope is that by recovering the primal experience of the sacred we may regain the religious commons we all share and end the contentious differences that have divided Christians, Jews, Muslims, Hindus, and Buddhists. Together we can attend to the flickering light of minor epiphanies that renew our sense of wonder, reverence, and other elemental emotions.

Articulating a renewed vision of the sacred will require the faith, hope, love, and actions of those from many generations acting in concert. What I offer here is no blueprint but mere glimpses. I trust that you who are joining me in the search for a new experience of the sacred in which to ground your lives will contribute different pieces of the puzzle. In time, a caring community will fit these fragments together to mold a vessel with which we may draw living water from the bottomless well of hope.

> Nothing that is worth doing can be achieved in a lifetime;
>   therefore we must be saved by hope.
> Nothing which is true or beautiful or good makes
>   complete sense in any immediate context of history;
>   therefore we must be saved by faith.
> Nothing we do, however virtuous, can be accomplished
>   alone; therefore we are saved by love.
>
> —REINHOLD NIEBUHR

A PREVIEW OF THE JOURNEY'S ITINERARY

Before we set out on our journey it would be wise to draw on wisdom that has guided pilgrims of the inward way for thousand of years. Joseph Campbell, the great cartographer of the journey of the mythological hero with a thousand faces, traced the path that so many have trodden for so long: from ego to spirit, from the profane to the sacred, from unquestioning life to wonder and re-enchantment. He explained that the journey involves three stages—separation, initiation, and return. The hero ventures forth from the world of every day (separation), goes into a region of supernatural wonders, and wins a decisive victory over demons and destructive forces with the aid of benevolent spirits and helpers (initiation). The selfless hero then brings his or her hard-earned wisdom back to the community of ordinary men and women.

In broad outline this is the journey we will be taking. But to understand what is involved in a modern heroic journey we need to translate the ancient language of mythology into the language of psychology. For us, confronting demons and slaying dragons means leaving the old order, forsaking the official authorities, and beginning a new life based on exploring our own experience, values, and visions. Our equivalent of trials, wandering in the labyrinth and wrestling with gods and demons, is the process of transcending our infantile ego (greed, fear, hatred, illusion) and the myths, values, and identities imposed on us by the authorities of our early years.

When we become disillusioned with our accepted religious and secular beliefs and lifestyles, we must create separation by setting forth into the desert (the place of initiation), where we will explore silence, solitude, and the difficult disciplines that lead to self-knowledge. After we have gained a new measure of self-understanding, we discover a hidden oasis. Here we remember our earliest intimations of the sacred, recover the elemental emotions exiled in the primal unconscious, and harness the power of epiphany to attain the jewel of compassion. We become the heroes in the dramatic narrative of our own lives. In the last stage of the journey (the return), we leave inner struggle behind and plunge back into communal life, where we explore new ways to speak about the unnamable G-d, create rituals that remind us to dwell reverentially on the earth, and join the perennial struggle for liberty and justice for all.

The story of the hero's journey is told as if it were a one-time adventure. In truth, it is unending. We receive many calls to adventure, and we will need to take leave of our old certainties, habits, and values again and again.

The journey is a spiral path that must be taken, or refused, time and time again.

This brief itinerary of the stages along the way will serve as a kind of handheld global positioning device that will allow us to keep track of our location.

2

The Desert: Retreat and Renewal

In order to come to a pleasure you have not,
you must go by a way that you will enjoy not.
To come to the knowledge that you have not,
you must go by a way that you know not.
To come to the possession you have not,
you must go by a way in which you possess not.
To come to be what you are not,
you must go by a way that you are not.

—JOHN OF THE CROSS

The Spirit immediately drove him out into the wilderness. And he was in the wilderness forty days, tempted by Satan; and he was with wild beasts; and the angels ministered to him.

—MARK 1:12

There is a common thread that runs through all religions, a belief that the way to spiritual renewal involves a retreat from "the world," an abandoning of our ordinary cultural values and lifestyles and an embracing of a life of austerity, asceticism, and self-denial. The great seers and mystics often lived in remote caves, ate little, and avoided all pleasures of the body. In an effort to rid themselves of the desires of the flesh they practiced self-flagellation, sleep deprivation, and prayer vigils. Before he became enlightened and adopted the middle path of moderation, the Buddha is said to have spent six years pushing his body to its limits, living on a single grain of rice a day and meditating constantly until he was nothing but skin and bones.

Tibetan monks in quest of enlightenment will often sit in freezing weather in the high Himalayas and cover themselves with wet robes, which they dry with body heat generated by their meditation. To this day, Trappist monks take vows of poverty, chastity, and obedience, give up speech, and live in a community that conducts its business in silence. In a more moderate vein, ordinary Catholics give up something for Lent, Jews fast during the high holy day of Yom Kippur, and Muslims are required during the month of Ramadan to abstain from food, sex, smoking, and drink from dawn to dusk.

In the past, the practice of austerity was a means of encouraging rigorous self-examination and confronting the selfish and destructive forces within the ego. Ancient lore and legend pictured the inner drama of the soul's struggle as occurring in a desert landscape filled with all manner of mythological demons, fiends, devils, and seductive temptations, as well as fearsome wild beasts.

Contemporary seekers are less likely to retreat to Death Valley, sit *zazen,* or practice self-denial. Our taste runs more to the sybaritic than the ascetic, more to Canyon Ranch than to Himalayan caves. We value spiritual renewal but not at the price of abstaining from our habitual pleasures. Nevertheless, the mythology of the desert quest encapsulates something essential to the renewal of our sense of the sacred, something we need to free from antiquity and translate into modern equivalents.

Our path may not lead to a hermit's life, but it must involve a retreat from the distractions of an overburdened style of life and a commitment to self-examination. For us, the vision quest that once led Native Americans to fast in solitude may take place in the office of a psychotherapist, in religious fellowship, in an hour we set aside for daily meditation, or in candid conversations with a trusted friend. And the austerities we practice may not require us to pray through the night, but they will involve refraining from excessive shopping, overeating, gossip, lying, arguing, hateful speech, substance abuse, and addiction to television, cell phones, or video games.

It is not difficult to translate the symbol of the

solitary quest into the psychological states and political events that reflect our current crisis, lost as we are in a desecrated economic, political, and ecological landscape. The widespread use of antidepressant drugs suggests that many of us, affluent or not, are troubled by what the early Christian fathers described as "the demon that walks at noonday"—melancholy, ennui, and anomie. Depression, anxiety, and despair are only the latest names we give to the feeling of living in an arid landscape from which the life-giving connection to the sacred has disappeared and the sense of personal meaning and vocation has vanished.

The great spiritual explorers of all ages and traditions have given us good but difficult advice—go into the desert, free yourself from the din, wrestle with your devils and come to know your better angels. Look squarely at your values and those of your society. Are you motivated more by a quest for profit, power, and possessions or by a desire to be kind, compassionate, and of service to others? If we have the courage to dwell on such questions, they will serve to encourage us, or lead us to despair of our condition and to embark on a renewed quest for G-d.

SOLITUDE

Escape from Established Religion and Cultural Mindmeld

Religion is what an individual does with his solitariness.

—ALFRED NORTH WHITEHEAD

Transformative thinking begins with a retreat into solitude. The great revolutions in religion, philosophy, and science would have been inconceivable without solitary thought experiments. Moses, Buddha, Jesus, and Muhammad spent long periods in agonizing self-examination before they arrived at their life-changing insights. Galileo's theory of planetary movement, Newton's discovery of gravity, Descartes's realization that clear and distinct ideas were the only guarantor of certainty (*Cogito ergo sum*), were all arrived at by men who were comfortable being alone with their thoughts. Einstein, whose thought experiments with space, time, and relativity were crucial to both the study of the cosmos and the study of subatomic particles, is famous for wandering around Princeton lost in thought. Once a friend who was making an appointment asked: "What time shall we meet?" "It doesn't matter," replied Einstein. "Any time between one o'clock and four o'clock will be fine. Whenever you get here I will be thinking."

A new animating vision of the sacred will come when and where it is least expected, from practices that run counter to the values that dominate our twenty-first-century global economic culture. The quest for such a vision begins by challenging the assurances of established religion and cultural ideology. Why? Because religion encompasses both the worst and the best human aspirations, our most conservative, authoritarian, fanatical impulses and our most liberal, revolutionary, open-minded urges. Every society is, in essence, a cult of the majority, a community that promises security and meaning to its citizens in exchange for a pledge of allegiance to the consensus values and the dominant mythology of the nation-state. A return to the root of the experience of the sacred will therefore have to be countercultural.

For instance, the theology of nationalism worships God and Country and demands that citizen soldiers be willing to kill or die when ordered to do so by secular authorities. Duty to the state supplants the dictates of individual conscience. It requires a cultural practice bordering on brainwashing to convert citizens into warriors, and a constant barrage of propaganda identifying the enemies of the nation as the enemies of God to condition us to support the killing of others. As a song from *South Pacific* tells us: "You've got to be taught, before it's too late, before you are six or seven or eight, to hate all the people your relatives hate." Aeschylus warned: "In war, truth is the first casualty." Patriotism may be a pivotal cultural virtue, but it is a dangerous seduction to those in search of perennial truths.

Spiritual renewal involves a radical change in identity, worldview, and lifestyle that can only blossom where solitude and silence allow us to listen to the still, small voice of G-d that is usually drowned out by the voices and values of our culture. Since culture makes addicts of us all, we must undergo a period of separation from the familiar before we can discover the sources of our uniqueness. An old Zen koan captures the difference between our cultural and our essential self with the seemingly nonsensical question "What was your face like before you were born?" Long before we arrive at the age of consent, culture superimposes a mask on our original face. We are indoctrinated and informed by the religion, ideology, myths, values, and organizing narratives of our parents and peers. In varying degrees, good citizens are sleepwalkers, unconsciously immersed in consensus reality, unquestioningly obedient to the story told by recognized cultural author-ities.

Separation from destructive secular values and addictive behaviors is the beginning of a spiritual 12-step program to break our addiction to the status quo—the unexamined religious myths and cultural narratives of our time—and to rehabilitate our capacity for experiencing the sacred nature of daily life.

There is a link between solitude, thought, and action that was well known to classical philosophers but has been nearly forgotten in modern times. The Roman Cato said of the solitary thinker, "Never is he more active than when he does nothing, never is he less alone than when he is by himself." It is only when we find the courage to question our comfortable ideas, values, beliefs, and myths that we can hear the voices and see the visions that give us hope, allowing us to return to society with a renewed sense of direction and purpose. In Hermann Hesse's novel *Siddhartha* the young prince, who has left a privileged existence to wander and meditate, returns to society after many years and applies for a job with a wealthy man. When he is asked what credentials his countercultural life has given him he replies: "I have learned to wait, to fast, and to think."

Fortunately, intrepid explorers from all ages have left us accounts of their spiritual adventures in solitude, and of the skills and disciplines they found necessary to survive. Their experiences provide examples of courage and wisdom that may help us escape the grip of the idolatrous gods and profane ideologies of our time. Listen to the stories of Gilgamesh, Buddha, Jesus, Lao-tzu, Abraham Lincoln, Martin Luther King Jr., Dorothy Day, Georgia O'Keeffe, and Mary Oliver, and you will hear echoes of a common story. The great autobiographical

explorers become our guides and companions as we share
their intimate experiences of suffering, anxiety, hope, joy,
freedom, and destiny. They tell us: Go alone into the
wilderness. Be leisurely. Stop, look, and listen. Confront
your demons, and welcome your nightmares. Know little, treasure your doubts. Discover your story. Learn to
love the questions. Quiet the mind and the tongue.

SILENCE

A Sanctuary Within the Void

Solitude is the gateway to silence. Be still and know.

Western culture seems to be a self-organizing conspiracy
against both solitude and silence. We are rapidly becoming enveloped in populous virtual realities, inundated
by a constant barrage of data. It is difficult to get away
from noise, pundits, propagandists, advertisers, cyber-
merchants, telemarketers, and telephone solicitors, all
hawking merchandise, ideologies, and gospels that promise fast cash, discounted merchandise, and cheap grace.

The money changers have colonized the kingdom of
silence. Within the global economy a quiet moment is an
underdeveloped resource, a wasted opportunity, an empty

lot on which something of value might be erected. Silence, like leisure, represents lost revenue. A Super Bowl minute is worth millions.

The absence of silence makes it almost impossible to appreciate the toll chatter and noise has taken on us. Omnipresent noise and speed destroy the fragile rhythms of meditative and contemplative thought. We literally can't hear ourselves think. We go from word to word instead of from silence to word. Our talk becomes babble, and listening a lost art.

To break free of this maelstrom of profanity and recover the clarity of the sacred we need a sanctuary of silence, a void into which we may retreat. Silence is our escape route from the cacophony of culture.

But silence can be threatening. Several years ago I led an Outward Bound expedition in the Big Bend region of Texas. After days of hiking and climbing we settled in a camp by the river and prepared to go on solo. Many of the participants were anxious about spending time in the desert with no distractions. When all the foot-weary men and women were safely settled in their isolated niches, I hiked to a spot I had chosen. I looked forward to getting away from the group for a while.

My refuge was a hollow at the foot of a cliff of white rock worn smooth by eons of springtime floods from the nearby stream that now was just a trickle. For the first hour or two I settled in, arranging my sleeping bag and rucksack with an eye to ways by which rattlesnakes might visit me in the night. Then I began to explore the rounded curves and small grottos of the water-worn rock. In the late afternoon I ran out of nest-building activities and sat by the stream. With nothing to do, I decided to do nothing. Just sit. A Zen saying came to mind: Sitting quietly, doing nothing, spring comes by itself.

Entering silence was not so easy. My sequestered valley was filled with the incessant chatter of a canyon wren, loud proclamations from a caucus of crows, water music, wind playing in the pinions, and the amplified whisper of an occasional passing jet. More disturbing was the noise inside my head. My mind was busy reviewing past triumphs and failures, engaging in dialogues with real and imaginary people, playing with erotic fantasies, and planning, planning, planning. Each time I tried to quiet the chatter it just got louder. With great effort I concentrated on the ragged rhythm of my breath, counting the inhalations and exhalations. But this only heightened my self-consciousness.

What, I wondered anxiously, would happen if I actually ceased striving, if I stepped out of the endless flow of words, explanations, and plans? There seemed to be a void lurking just below my carefully constructed personality. Death and nothingness lay waiting in ambush. My fears turned Descartes's moment of enlightenment on its head: I don't think; therefore I am not.

Slowly I surrendered, and allowed the unacceptable thought of death—my death—to remain in my awareness. As I did, a corridor opened into primal emotions, feelings as old as history and as universal as humankind. I felt the fear of the unknown and gnawing questions I could neither answer nor dismiss: Where have I come from? What happens to me after I die? What is this no-thing-ness that is my origin and my destiny?

My mind played with explanations, myths, and beliefs, but none satisfied me. I could find nothing to hold on to, no rock in the stream of time. As I invited my fear to linger, it turned its other face toward me—the tragic grief for all that is fleeting. Job knew: "Man is like the grass of the field. The wind passes over it, and it is gone, and its place knows it no more."

Unexpectedly, mourning the momentary marvel of my own life released me from self-absorption. I felt blessed and cleansed. Exhausted, I lay under a tree. Perhaps I dozed. A vast horizon surrounded me, filled only by antiphonal winds. The moment lasted a delicious, eternal instant before I began to try to understand it; immediately the silence evaporated and my ego jumped back into command.

Who was I during those moments when there was only the wind in the trees?

Here.

Today.

Empty.

No thing to say.

Blessed silence.

SLAYING THE SPEED DEMON
Holy Leisure

Be leisurely
And know G-d,

Speed is the evil twin of noise.
Leisure is the bride of silence.

—SANDOR McNAB

The Greeks recognized two modes of time, *chronos* and *kairos*. *Chronos* brings us the time measured by watches, clocks, and calendars. It is linear, uniform, and as predictable as the tick of your grandfather's clock, an arrow flying perpetually from the present moment into the future. Within the well-marked units of chronological time, agreements are made, contracts are formed, and the business of the public is conducted.

The second mode of time, *kairos,* is organic, rhythmic, cyclical, intimate, and bodily. In the right moment, in the *kairos,* a woman gives birth, a man dies in the fullness of his years, winter yields its icy grip to the soft breezes of spring, grief gives way to gratitude, anger runs its course, and forgiveness blossoms. According to Ecclesiastes, the essence of wisdom is knowing how to tell time. "To everything there is a season, and a time to every purpose under heaven. A time to be born and a time to die, a time to plant and a time to pluck up that which is planted." Or, as they say in Las Vegas, "a time to hold 'em, and a time to fold 'em."

It is within the leisurely movement of *kairos* that we learn the lessons of dreams, mark the passages from one stage of life to another, and measure the growth of faith, hope, and love. In the New Testament, *kairos* refers to the moments in which God breaks into history, making an appearance through the prophets or Jesus. In a wider sense, it is any moment when an ordinary event becomes an epiphany.

Back in the 1970s Herbert Marcuse assured us in *Eros and Civilization* that we were on the edge of a leisure revolution; soon we wouldn't need to work more than twenty hours a week. The wealth created by our machines would, at long last, usher in the age of Aquarius so we could play, express our creativity in the arts, and let eros run free.

But things didn't turn out that way. Increasingly, the

industrial world was being held hostage by the Speed Demon. We created time-motion studies so we could measure efficiency to the nearest second and began living by the clock. We proudly exhibited the new symbol of our devotion to the great god Chronos on our wrists. Time became equated with money, and more money with speed. The demands of the competitive market drove the pace of life at an ever-escalating rate. Hurry up. You are already a day late and a dollar short. To the speedy belong the spoils. Be a Ten-Minute Manager.

Tyrannized by the demands of commerce and instantaneous communication, we began to lose our sense of sweet leisure and the graceful rhythms of personal time. Almost all of us became addicted to the speedy and demanding style of life that allowed pharmaceutical companies to make billions from stress-reducing drugs. Increasingly, high-speed populations colonized low-speed populations and forced them to abandon life cued to the circadian rhythms of the body and replace it with the frantic pace demanded by economic competition.

Ultimately, our addiction to speed cannot be solved by Prozac. Yet there is good news: we are bio-mythic animals, and when myths change we change with them. But what is required of us is nothing less than conversion to a worldview that runs counter to that of *homo economicus*.

Speed is the essence of profane time. Sacred time is polymorphous, a many-splendored thing. It produces a

calmer nervous system, a more harmonious balance between waking and dreaming life. It weaves past, present,
and future (memory, awareness, and hope) into a coherent narrative.

One of my most memorable experiences of sacred
time took place when I met an old temple keeper while I
was traveling through the Himalayan mountain kingdom
of Bhutan. As we sat together for an evening around a
campfire, he explained through an interpreter how he
made amulets to drive away certain diseases and keep jeal-
ous demons at bay. He did not aspire to be reborn as a
priest but hoped he had accumulated enough good karma
to be reborn in Bhutan. He could not imagine wanting to
be anywhere other than where he was. As we talked, I
kept glancing at his hands. They seemed almost supernat-
urally still, and I realized that I had never in my life been
as peaceful and as firmly settled in my place as he was.

What, I asked myself, would happen if I let the rising
and setting of the sun and moon mark the parameters of
my day? If I attended to the changing colors, smells, and
textures and allowed them to inform me about the
progress of the seasons? What if the scent of lilacs reminded me that spring brings the perennial promise of
rebirth? If flaming maples or golden aspen warned me to
prepare for the coming darkness of a shorter day?

It is easy to identify the sense of living in an eternal
now in a temple keeper or a child, but what does that in-

sight offer me? What does it demand of me? How might I, in the chaos of my modern life, learn to remain in a state of intense stillness?

MEETINGS WITH DARK ANGELS
Repentance and Confession

This is the very perfection of man, to find out his own imperfections.

—SAINT AUGUSTINE

The secular wisdom of the moment encourages cultivation of an extroverted lifestyle. It counsels us to be optimistic, stay on the sunny side, keep busy, and forget our past mistakes. By contrast, ancient wisdom encourages us to welcome our darkest dreams and memories into the full light of consciousness.

Alone in the profound darkness of the desert night we are threatened by shadowy beings and vague emotions whose forms we cannot discern. Wild beasts. Demons. Phantoms of betrayed conscience. Memories of failure. Betrayal by those we love. Even our well-defended egos are helpless against the onslaught that originates deep in our unconscious. When accused and called upon to confess and repent, the ego's normal response is to deny, rationalize, and direct guilt onto some Other—a husband, wife, enemy, or devil.

A retreat to the desert forces us to consider how the self and the nation are guilty of greed, aggression, cruelty, and indifference. Two paths diverge and we must choose which to follow.

The Secular Path	*The Sacred Path*
taken by the ego,	taken by the higher self,
by nations and institutions,	by communities of concern,
operates from a perspective	is animated by a spirit
of paranoia, self-righteousness.	of metanoia, or repentance.
We are (I am) right	We were (I was)
in my beliefs.	uncaring, unimaginative.
They are wrong, guilty,	We are all flawed
malevolent, hostile.	creatures, imperfect.
We must defend ourselves.	Please forgive us.

Scientific knowledge and pure information can be passed from one person to another without self-revelation or repentance. But the type of wisdom we get from friendship and love that may heal body, mind, and spirit involves vulnerability, self-knowledge, and the willingness to examine one's shadow—to practice the virtue of metanoia. The partners in any intimate relationship will wound each other in a hundred small ways, requiring them to confess their failures and ask for forgiveness. Certainly the dumbest nine words ever spoken about love are those from the film *Love Story*— "Love means never having to say you're sorry." (The nine-word aphrodisiac: "I was wrong. I am sorry. Please forgive me.")

Jesus advised us to remove the beam in our own eye before we try to remove it from someone else. Freud insisted that it was essential for psychotherapists to undergo psychotherapy as part of their training. Our awareness of our brokenness is the prelude to renewal, the first of the steps that lead to breaking our addiction to the ego's perspective. Every religious tradition teaches that the path to spiritual maturity passes through the valley of the shadow and the dark night of the soul.

Typically, nations, institutions, and corporations do not admit to their mistakes and repent, but after World War II, Germany went through an extraordinary period of examining its war crimes, death camps, and genocide. Its expression of remorse led to the healing resolve to keep the memory of infamy alive in order to guard against repetition. In Japan the process was quite the opposite. Generation after generation of Japanese leaders have refused to acknowledge the rape of Nanking, the kidnapping of women who were consigned to the sexual needs of soldiers, or the atrocities perpetrated against the Korean people. Nor has the United States ever repented for the firebombings of Dresden and Tokyo, or for the use of atomic weapons against Hiroshima and Nagasaki. Had we engaged in a prolonged period of honest repentance for the two million lives lost in Vietnam, we might have decided against invading Afghanistan and Iraq. Our inability to acknowledge our mistakes condemns us to repeat them.

When we confess our personal failures and repent for our complicity in the sins of our community, we learn the comforting lesson of humility. As the ancient creed taught, we must be crucified, dead and buried, before we rise again to new life. Hope sleeps silently in the humus, waiting for the hard shell of the ego—pride, self-righteousness, and the will to power—to be cracked open.

I confess:

I am a member of the gang of ecological bandits that has participated in the pollution and destruction of the environment of my fellow humans and other sentient beings. I wantonly enjoy an unjust share of the gifts of the earth and ignore the plight of the powerless and the poor. I have plundered the heritage of my children.

I am the citizen of a nation that expends its precious resources to maintain the largest and most heavily armed

military in human history. I have acquiesced to the un-
lawful overthrow of foreign governments, to the bombing
of civilian populations, and to the waging of unjust, pre-
emptive wars. I have remained silent as my country has
committed crimes against humanity and has refused to
submit to the international rule of law.

I suffer from the disease of concupiscence—endless
desire. I am never satisfied with what I have, even though
I am drowning in things I do not need. I buy. I consume.
Therefore, I exist.

I excuse myself from facing the fate of the downtrodden with the comforting theory that poverty is a struc-
tural problem that cannot be solved by the generosity of
wealthy nations. I have turned my eyes aside so that I
need not see the evil done by those who have acted in my
name, who have used my tax dollars to keep me safe from
the amorphous threat of terrorism. I have watched while
the civil rights upon which my country was founded have
been eroded and the international standards of the
Geneva Conventions have been violated.

Of these things I repent.

Far from being debilitating, the guilt and shame involved in honest confession and repentance is a testimony to the transcendent element in human identity, to
the sacred core. It is an acknowledgment that our lives
stand before the judgment of the collective conscience,

whose jurisdiction transcends the laws, morals, ethics, and customs of tribe and nation. The golden rule, the categorical imperative, and the bodhisattva vow—all rest on the recognition that we become fully human only when we treat others as full members of our universal community.

The voices of guilt and shame that spoke to us in the desert night become our Dark Angels, our pathfinders and guides. The great triad—confession/repentance/forgiveness—remains a central feature of religion because, as philosopher Hannah Arendt puts it, the power to forgive "is the one miracle-working faculty of man, the faculty that allows us to act rather than be caught in endless repetition of the cycles of violence and revenge."

One of the most powerful parables of confession, repentance, and renewal we have witnessed in our time emerged from the work of the Truth and Reconciliation Commission in South Africa. It was only when the architects and enforcers of apartheid confessed their cruel and evil deeds in open court that the process of healing between victims and perpetrators of violence could begin. Compassion grows from the realization that I can only forgive my neighbor for the injuries I have suffered when I can forgive myself for the injuries I have caused. W. H. Auden put it this way: "You shall love your crooked neighbor with your crooked heart."

A confession has to be part of your new life.

—LUDWIG WITTGENSTEIN

BLESSED DOUBT
The Virtues of Agnosticism

To know that you do not know is the best.
To pretend to know when you do not know is a disease.

—LAO-TZU

In the desert the eye strains in vain to see beyond the endless horizon. But there is only sand, the sky, and the eternal void. Longing for sheltering palms and cool waters where there are none, the theological imagination creates all manner of phantasmagorical kingdoms. By contrast, the agnostic mind refuses all wishful thinking.

Agnosticism is as old as thoughtfulness, but it was Thomas Henry Huxley who invented the term *agnostic* in the 1840s to distinguish himself from theologians who professed to provide divinely revealed answers to the most profound questions, such as: Does God exist? How can we know Him? Why would He create evil, and why do the good suffer and the wicked prosper? According to

Huxley, the theologians "were quite sure that they had more or less successfully solved the problem of existence; while I was quite sure I had not, and had a pretty strong conviction that the problem was insoluble."

Agnosticism, which does not preclude or accept religious belief but takes a middle ground, is a form of epistemological humility, an acknowledgment of the essential limits of human knowledge. No matter the startling discoveries of astrophysics, neurophysiology, and quantum mechanics, agnostics remind us that we are no nearer to understanding the ultimate whys and wherefores of our existence. A millennium from now we will have solved a multitude of theoretical and practical problems, but the mystery of being will remain. Human beings will always live under what the medieval Christian mystic Jakob Böhme called "the cloud of Unknowing." In the court of reason, the millions of orthodox believers who blindly accept the authority of ancient scriptures and the pronouncements of religious authorities have no standing.

Don't confuse agnosticism with atheism—the denial of the existence of God, whether it is the God of Judaism, Christianity, or Islam or G-d the indefinable creative intelligence that is within and beyond all knowable existence. It is impossible, by definition, to know whether a God defined as a supernatural being transcending time and space even exists, much less to have any knowledge about such an entity. But, as we will see, this does not prevent us from using the idea of an unknown G-d who remains forever beyond the reach of our finite intelligence, nor of experiencing the full range of elemental sacred emotions.

At its best, agnosticism is adventurous thinking rooted in the courage to doubt revealed truth, commonly accepted opinions, and cultural myths. It is about honoring our doubts and affirming our ignorance of those ultimate matters on which theologians and anti-theologians pontificate with such certainty. In a spirit of courageous inquiry, agnosticism is willing to challenge authority, break taboos, and live with disapproval and criticism. Above all, it is ludic, a playful way of thinking that finds delight in paradox and contradiction and the imagination's tendency toward endless speculation. We do not know, therefore we play. Our ignorance is our certainty; our openness is our treasure.

VERBAL FASTING
A Moratorium on Hallowed Words

When the world began
God, they say, created man.
Conversely,
Dancing around the sod,
Man, they say, created God.
Watch your words, or they may do
Something of the kind to you.

—UNKNOWN

Sometimes, nothin' can be a real cool hand.

—LUKE JACKSON, IN *COOL HAND LUKE*

As bio-mythic, storytelling animals, we inevitably construct a linguistic frame around objects, events, and emotions. Language is our glory and our downfall, our greatest freedom and our maximum-security prison. Before we know it, the gossamer words we have spun to capture our fleeting experience harden into rigid beliefs that block the flow of passing moments and new meanings.

Our most hallowed languages and symbols—the religious and political terms that encode the dominant myths of our culture—establish a tyrannical hold on our minds, emotions, and imaginations. Before we know it, our unthinking allegiance to the God who blesses "democracy," "capitalism," and "freedom" becomes a rationale for forcing our way of life on others, whom we define as "enemies" when they resist. Unknowingly, our spirits become colonized by the voices and values of officials, authorities, and pundits.

Once the spin doctors, advertisers, propagandists, and religious authorities lay claim to language, the sacred connection between word and truth is severed. The common trust upon which all civil society depends—the understanding that we will tell the truth and abide by our word—is destroyed. When systematic lying, dissimulation, and secrecy become a way of life, the public ceases to expect the truth from government officials and cynicism blossoms.

Every institution and profession—religious or secular—has its lingo. It is the nature of professions and organizations to invent special languages that are understood by insiders but are otherwise opaque; to be a professional is to speak in code. For the uninitiated, reading a political policy brief, a theological text, a legal document, a medical diagnosis, or a journal article on structuralism is like deciphering code. It is not uncommon for professionals of all kinds—lawyers, politicians, businesspeople, pastors, and priests—to use obfuscation, complexity, and mystification to claim knowledge—and thereby power—unavailable to the layperson.

In the beginning of the Christian era it was said that spirit became flesh. But then Spirit became Word (logos), and words became sacrament, which in turn became the basis for the church. The farther Christianity moved from its original event, the more powerfully theology established its dominion over the living spirit. The creed makers performed a reverse miracle: They turned wine into water.

How can we break the spell of religious language, wake up from the hypnosis of god jargon, and escape from the gravitational pull of the political ideologies implicit in Judaism, Christianity, and Islam?

The first antidote for the prostitution of language is voluntary chastity. Just say no. Paul Tillich, the Protestant theologian, said that the great words—*faith, hope, love, grace, sin,* and *salvation*—sometimes become so trivialized and degraded that we need to cease using them for a generation. We need to declare a moratorium on old, hallowed, and overused words: a linguistic fast.

Mystics within the great religious traditions have always cautioned against becoming too comfortable with language describing G-d. Judaism prohibited naming G-d altogether. What theologians called the *via negativa* suggests that we remain most faithful to the ultimate mystery when we remember what G-d is not. The One we try to capture in our names and definitions remains, as Martin Luther said, a hidden G-d.

One way to recover the original meaning and power of religion is to adopt the radical discipline of linguistic asceticism. Put yourself on an austere verbal fast: slim down; clean house. During the month of Ramadan, good Muslims do not eat between dawn and dusk. Abstaining from our habitual patterns of eating and speaking sharpens the appetite *and* the tongue.

Stop using the tattered language, outworn creeds, and tired metaphors that were once vital but now belong in museums of ancient beliefs. Abandon archaic notions that no longer speak to our condition. The primitive idea that we can be purified by the blood sacrifice of an animal, or a savior who vicariously atones for our sins, makes no more sense to the modern mind than a three-level universe with heaven above and hell below.

What would happen if churches, synagogues, and mosques underwent a time of verbal fasting, when they put their old stories and traditional religious languages on hiatus? At first things would probably get worse. People wouldn't know how to talk about religious matters. But gradually congregations would begin to experiment with new metaphors and create a new poetry of faith by sharing stories and by helping one another discover fresh expressions of their perennial fears and hopes.

Years ago, when I first took my own advice, I made a list of religious, political, and psychological words I habitually used and forced myself to give them up: *neurosis, paranoia, salvation, justification by faith, grace, sin, estrangement, mysticism, spirituality, faith, hope, vocation,* et cetera. (I told my children I would put one dollar in a box every time I slipped—a costly agreement.) I stopped praying, stopped reading religious literature, and stopped going to church. Insofar as I was able, I allowed the old words to be replaced by silence.

At first, I became anxious. The silence was painfully awkward. Stripped of familiar language, the God I had known disappeared from the horizon of my life, leaving me feeling naked and vulnerable. Without this God, my basic values and core sense of identity were thrown into question.

Gradually, the silence took on a different valence. God was replaced by G-d. The threatening emptiness turned into sweet anticipation, like that of a lover waiting quietly for the object of her desire to appear. The fear I had experienced suddenly appeared baseless, even comical. How, I wondered, had I fallen prey to the absurd belief that the One with Ten Thousand Names could only exist within my limited religious vocabulary? It seemed unlikely that the Unknowable One would starve to death if I neglected to make the old burnt offerings.

(It would be interesting to see what would happen within corporations if, for one hundred days, it was forbidden to talk about profits, losses, stockholders, competition, or market share. Some workers might wonder out loud if what they were doing with fifty or sixty hours a week truly reflected how they wished to spend their fleeting years. Others might wonder whether the product

being promoted was ecologically viable, or if their contri-
bution to a global economy was likely to benefit those on
the planet who needed it most, or whether we might
choose to measure the success of our society by gross national happiness [as they do in Bhutan], rather than by
gross national product.)

THE NEVER-ENDING JOURNEY
Loving the Questions

In the desert nothing is exactly what it seems. A distant
lake shimmers for a moment, promising relief and re-
freshment, but as you draw closer it vanishes. Sandstorms
obscure the sun and cause the unwary traveler to walk in
circles. Springs and oases that were once verdant dry up
and disappear beneath the shifting sands. To live in the
desert is to become part of an unending quest for water
and wild game. To join any new quest we must challenge
the values and concerns that have governed our lives to
this time.

Freud got it slightly wrong. True, many of us suffer
from the thorn in the flesh of childhood wounds, but we
suffer more frequently from a void, from what hasn't happened to us, from what we haven't found as a result of the
questions we haven't asked.

Questioning is not something we do but something

we are—an elemental force. Were you to dissect my brain, you would find that the neurochemical circuitry, the complex strands of cells that make up my brain and my mind, are as individual as my fingerprints. But beyond the wetware, what makes me Sam Keen rather than Rupert Murdoch are the questions that shape my life. Instead of spending each day asking myself how I could acquire more news media, I wonder about the vagaries of the experience of the sacred and the shape of future religion.

Nothing shapes our lives so much as the questions we ask, refuse to ask, or never dream of asking. Our minds, bodies, feelings, and relationships are literally informed by our questions. The defining essence of an individual is his or her quest print. The men and women who made an enduring mark in history, for better and for worse, ignored the accepted worldviews, values, and myths of their time and chose to pursue their own answers to their deepest questions.

Here's a random sample.

How can we put an end to suffering?—Buddha
What is eternal and unchanging?—Plato
What is the will of God?—Jesus
Of what may I be certain?—Descartes
How is a falling apple like a rising moon?—Sir Isaac
    Newton

Why were men born free but are everywhere in
    chains?—Karl Marx
What is the meaning of dreams?—Sigmund Freud
How can we create a master race?—Adolf Hitler
Does God play dice with the universe?—Albert
    Einstein
How is a woman unlike a man?—Betty Friedan

The questions we habitually ask determine whether
we will be superficial or profound, acceptors of the status
quo or searchers, creators of the peace between nations
or the cause of its destruction. They reflect our values,
needs, circumstances, and situation. It is the courage to
ponder the great mythic questions that gives depth to
human life. These queries form antibodies that protect us
from the diseases of orthodoxy and ideology, although
sometimes they lead us to create new pseudo religions,
such as fascism or communism. But so long as we return
again and again to the great unanswerable questions, we
will never wander far from the endless sky and quicken-
ing winds of the spirit.

And if we don't?

If I don't ask, "What are my gifts?" and "What is my
vocation?" I may spend my life working at a job that has
little or no meaning for me. If I don't ask myself, "Am I
willing to kill the designated enemies of my government?" I may join the military, and possibly be placed

in a combat situation where my only choice is to kill or be killed. If I don't ask, "Should I compromise my values to serve the interests of my employer?" I am more likely to tailor my personality to what is demanded for advancement. If I do not ask, "Who am I? What is my story?" I am more likely to be informed by the myths, scripts, and stereotypes of my culture. If I don't ask, "What do I believe about G-d and the ultimate purpose of life?" I am more likely to live unconsciously, within either a profane ideology or an uncritical religious orthodoxy.

To be authentically religious is not to affirm any one creed or to have unwavering faith in a transcendent God. It is to be passionately concerned with the meaning of existence, and to linger with questions of origin, destination, and purpose, not because they are answerable but because we are swept up by our cultural myths when we cease to ask these questions.

These perennial, unanswerable questions send us forth on a philosophical quest that lasts a lifetime:

Origins: Why is there something rather than nothing? What is the origin of life? Of my life?

Destination: What is the end toward which history and my life are moving? Who or what is the moving force?

Death: For what may I hope when I die? Is there life after death? Immortality of the soul? Resurrection of the body? Reincarnation? Complete annihilation?

Identity: Who am I? How do I become that unique self that fulfills my destiny? How do I win my freedom from biological necessity and from the myth my culture has imposed over my body, mind, and spirit?

Vocation: Does my life have meaning? If so, what is it? How do I contribute to life beyond my own?

Community: Who are my people? With whom do I belong? Do I have enemies? If so, who are they?

Authority: Who is in charge? Who is the author of my story? What are the rules? What am I obligated to do? Why?

Path of life: What is the map of life—the stages along the way? How should I conduct myself as a child, an adolescent, an adult, and an elder?

Evil: Why is there evil? Why do the good suffer and the evil prosper sometimes? Or vice versa? Is there ultimate justice? What can I do to reduce the power of evil?

> *Dis-ease:* What is wrong with me? With human be-
> ings? Why does dis-ease exist? Pain? Why are we
> self-destructive sometimes?

> *Healing:* What is wholeness, health? What nostrums,
> medicines, means of healing are available? Who
> can help, who can heal?

> *G-d:* Are we alone in the universe? Is there a supra-
> human caring intelligence?

In the beginning, the prodigal son was comfortable in
the household of his father. He accepted and practiced
the ancient faith. But one day his spirit was disturbed by
questions neither he nor his elders could answer. Leaving home on a quest for answers, he wandered in the
desert and in the distant land of the skeptics and flesh-
pots. Often on cold nights among strangers, he longed
to return to the warmth and security of home and put
aside his doubts. But his questions would not be si-
lenced. They resounded in his mind like the beat of a
great drum in a vast emptiness.

In time, haunted and exhausted by finding no path
that led back to the innocent land in which he had
once lived, he fell into despair and decided to abandon
his quest. But some impulse encouraged him to keep
going, and gradually he resigned himself to being an
anxious pilgrim on a road whose destination he did not

know. Then, one night in a foreign land, he realized with the clarity of a star falling in a moonless sky that his agonizing questions had become his treasure, his joy, and his guide to a never-ending adventure in a desert, an oasis, and a wondrous world that had become his home.

3

The Hidden Oasis

※

*What makes the desert beautiful is that somewhere it
hides a well.*

—Antoine de Saint-Exupéry

It happened a long time ago, in one of the darkest periods
of my life. I had resigned my professorship, divorced the
wife of my youth, and was living alone in San Francisco,
fifteen hundred miles from my children. In those days my
major preoccupation was trying to figure out what was
wrong with me. Why was I always anxious? Why was I so
painfully self-obsessed? It seemed that the more I practiced
the disciplines of self-examination, doubt, and asceticism
that should have led me to greater self-awareness and acceptance, the deeper I sank into depression.

One day I received a postcard from a wise friend,
Rabbi Zalmon Schachter. The card said: "You're probably
wondering why your friends are beginning to gather

around you. I know you feel you're stuck in a dark place. But if you knew where a chrysalis was about to break free of the cocoon and become a butterfly, wouldn't you rush to the place where it was happening? What your friends see that you do not (yet) is that you are emerging."

The card was a bolt of lightning into the heart of my darkness. Was I about to emerge into a new day? The very possibility that I was in the process of metamorphosis filled me with hope. Perhaps a week later, I woke in the middle of the night with the awareness that something strange was happening. It was as if the northern lights somehow had become incarnate in my flesh, as if each color of the rainbow was charged with a different erotic sensation that traveled up and down the length of my body. Light, pleasure, and joy formed a seamless synthesis, and I felt the delight of yielding to something that overpowered my critical mind. I lay very still for an indeterminate time, savoring the sensation before falling back into sleep. I awoke early, completely refreshed, knowing that Zalmon had been right. I was finally emerging into the light. Now, thirty-seven years later, I mark that night as the moment that I began to move toward a hidden oasis, where I would find benevolent spirits and helpers and recover the elemental emotions that would initiate me in the presence of the sacred.

•   •   •

At first the path leading to an oasis is nearly imperceptible. A slight veering away from the arid landscape and the painful disciplines of self-examination, doubt, and asceticism. A turning toward the promise of transformation—the redolence of green fields and flowering trees coming from a yet-unseen wellspring of life.

The transformation that begins in the desert occurs in the inner spiritual landscape and does not immediately alter the facts of our quotidian existence. A wide variety of metaphors have been used to describe the experience.

It is as if:

the darkness becomes luminous;
we are surprised by joy;
anxiety gives way to courage;
we are healed of our dis-ease;
we are fully alive although we are still destined to die;
our defense mechanisms are disarmed, and we dare
    to be vulnerable in a dangerous world;
we regain an innocent eye;
we are born again;
a chrysalis is emerging from the cocoon.

These metaphors of awakening, enlightenment, and metamorphosis point to momentary peak experiences of transcendence. But William James warned us that, while it is notoriously easy to have religious experiences, it is difficult to create a religious life. So, before considering how we craft a religious life by re-owning our elemental emotions, learning to speak in poetic ways about G-d, and practicing justice, we turn our attention to those largely fleeting experiences in which we have premonitions that we are encompassed within a sacred web that includes all sentient beings. These minor oases are memories of Edenic moments of childhood; a sudden feeling of being quickened or enthusiastic (possessed by a god); momentary epiphanies and visions.

REMEMBERING EDEN

I remember a time when my world was magical and every moment was charged with a sense of the numinous. Twice upon a time, long ago and far away, I inhabited a garden of innocent delight and sacred pleasure. Before my fall into Presbyterian religion and modern profanity I lived in a seamless world, with no clear boundaries between time and eternity, self and other, sacred and profane. I was six years old and there was only Now and Forever.

I remember staring into the mirror, seeing the stranger's eyes of my reflected self and asking, "Who are you? Where have you come from? Why are you here?" I knew even then that I, the knower, could never be known to myself.

I remember sitting on my father's lap, secure forever,

beyond the realm of death, feeling the vibrations of his rich baritone voice singing "Danny Boy," keeping time with the beat of my heart.

I remember lying on my back outdoors on moonlit summer evenings, watching the endless drift of cloud castles, formed solely for my amusement.

I remember waking on dark nights when the chorus of cicadas was suddenly interrupted by ominous rustling sounds in the backyard. Bears? Burglars? (As it turned out, it was only the insomniac next door, Mr. Traylor, wandering in quest of elusive sleep.)

I remember rearranging rocks in small creeks to produce an elaborate symphony of water music—babble, ripple, gurgle, whoosh.

I remember perfectly ordinary mornings when everything seemed charged with anticipation, a kind of pervasive Christmas spirit, as if some extraordinary surprise awaited me around every shrub and tree.

THE QUICKENED LIFE

It happens suddenly. Deadness gives way to new life. Depression lifts and the imagination begins to play in the fields of the Lord, to entertain novel possibilities. Unexpectedly, the chains fall away and we are surprised to find ourselves free to experience vivid life. Slowly, carefully as a surgeon guiding a laser scalpel, we peel away the layers of cultural myths, roles, and assigned identities that deaden our capacity to live and touch the quick—the core of our being.

> **Quicken:** to make alive, to vivify, to revive or resuscitate, as from death or an inanimate state, hence, to excite, to stimulate, to impart additional energy. *Quicken* chiefly stresses the renewal of suspended life or growth or the arousing to full activity, usually suddenly.
>
> —*Webster's New International Dictionary*

It has been said: Jesus came to separate the quick from the dead, the spirit from the letter, the living heart of religion from its deadening husks, the nut from the shell. A radical notion! Beneath the nail, beneath the shell, beneath the character armor that protects us from life, lies the region of maximum sensitivity. The quick is the holy ground, the place where we are most alive, where we touch the great mystery of our existence.

> Don't ask what the world needs. Ask what makes you come alive and go out and do it. Because what the world needs is people who have come alive.
>
> —Howard Thurman

EPIPHANIES AND SACRED VISIONS

In the twinkling of an eye
the world changes faces.
Apocalypse, epiphany or shape-shifting.

We experience the world as both ordinary and numinous. An epiphany is an event that flips the switch, changing our vision from profane to sacred in a conversion that may be momentary or last a lifetime.

My neighbor has observed a young male mountain lion crossing the lower part of my farm near the place where the stream backs up against cliffs whose volcanic outcroppings, like the changing shapes of clouds, can assume many forms, depending on the light. I have a near-obsessive, frustrated desire to catch a glimpse of the wary cat. In the dusky late afternoon, as I am walking through the tangle of bay and brush, I suddenly see the magnificent animal crouched in a large pocket of the cliff. I strain my eyes. Why isn't he moving, trying to escape? Instantly, he disappears. Or did he magically become that low-lying bush swaying in the breeze? A moment ago I could see no bush. Now I can see no lion.

I stand in the checkout line of the supermarket, feeling grumpy in my hurry to get home. The clerk makes small talk with the grocery bagger. Self-righteously, I snap at her: "I don't have all day." Then I look at her closely for the first time, noticing the tightness in her neck and the unmistakable hint of sadness in her eyes. Instantly, the anonymous functionary before me becomes a person I recognize as a human being worthy of reverence. I say, "I'm sorry I snapped at you."

"That's okay," she replies with a smile. "It's been that kind of day for me too."

Sacred vision is a trickster, a clown, a changeling. In a flash it transforms a lion into a bush, an "it" into a "thou." Like the gestalt puzzle of the goblet/woman, no sooner does it show us a figure than it reveals the ground that makes the figure disappear. We cannot see both at the same time. In an instant the picture changes, although every detail remains the same. Hide and seek. Now you see it, now you don't. The sacred and the profane are always playing musical chairs.

Sacred vision reveals no fact that is not available to secular investigation. No miracles. No supernatural events. No explanations. No special knowledge. If Buddha was virgin-born, or if the body of Christ was physically resurrected and went on a postmortem walkabout through the Holy Land, then theology might be considered a science that deals with miraculous facts. But if believers and unbelievers inhabit the same world but experience and interpret it differently, theology can only be an art, like poetry or music, expressing the poignancy of living in a sacred world that evades our simplistic explanations.

Paul Tillich, the famous theologian, liked to tell the story of a small boy riding in the country with his father. The boy sees some animals grazing in the field and asks: "What are those?" "Cows," replies the father. "Why?" asks the boy. Both boy and father were looking at the same animal, but one was caught up in the secular mode of objective seeing, the other in the reverential mode of wonder. Why should there be cows? Why was there something in the field rather than nothing?

Every epiphany, whether triggered by the sudden awareness of the intricate design of the eye, the starry sky above, the moral law within, or the charismatic person of Jesus or Muhammad, points to the same ineffable sense that the world is sacred and ultimately beyond our understanding. When scientists have answered all the questions about how cows evolved, we are still left to wonder why there are cows at all.

The alchemy of epiphany is beyond explanation. At the heart of the experience is something unutterable, unnamable, filled with power. In that blinding moment when an ordinary aspen, a tree I have habitually taken for granted, is set aflame by the golden light of what can only be a numinous presence, I awaken to the marvel of being. Nothing external has happened, yet everything has changed as I contemplate the presence just revealed to me.

Epiphanies occur at a specific time and place. Because they happen to one person at a time, epiphanies, and the elemental emotions that accompany them, are always embedded in personal narratives and autobiographies. Those sacred moments that startle, illumine, challenge, and encourage us may well seem meaningless to an outsider, like the private language of lovers. There is no way we can truly convey to anyone else what happens to us in those encounters in which we find the world unaccountably changed. But we can tell the story.

Many years ago I received a letter from a woman I did not know. "I am a forty-two-year-old woman. I've never received a love letter, never received flowers from a man. I have attempted suicide and have contemplated it many times since. And yet, these wonders I have known: a maple tree in autumn, each leaf exactly the color of gold; a weed-like microcosm whose perfect petals are no bigger than the head of a pin. The dawning of each season with its own unique perfume, spring and autumn bringing the strongest scents. These and many other moments of grace have kept me going. God is in the details. The same spirit that animates the flower animates me. We are in the right place, right here and now. We don't need to aspire to heaven."

Like birth, death has a way of initiating us into the

awe-filled dimension of the mystery of being. On November 4, 1964, knowing my father was gravely ill, I flew from Louisville, Kentucky, to Prescott, Arizona, hoping to see him while he was still alive. A friend met me at the airport with the news that Dad had died a few hours earlier. Forty-five years later the grief lingers in my heart. So does the glory. Autumn in Arizona was a riot of burnished gold dying into winter. And I understood beyond all doubt that beauty is fleeting and its loss leaves an incurable ache in the heart of our mortality.

To experience our lifescape as sacred also creates a moral paradox. How can we both revere and use the world? Whatever is seen as sacred is, at least in principle, inviolate. It ought to be hallowed, venerated as an end rather than a means. But clearly this is not always possible. If I am to survive the winter, my glorious, molten aspen may need to be harvested for firewood, and I may need to kill one of the graceful deer who so delight me during warmer months. Among traditional hunters and gatherers, the game animal upon which they depended for food was believed to have sacrificed itself during a successful hunt. The Bushmen of South Africa performed a ritual dance reenacting the kill and thanking the eland for its life. They believed that through this sacrament their prey returned to earth to sustain the herd.

In premodern times, shedding blood through hunting and warfare was considered a tragic necessity, requiring

repentance and purification. The modern worldview tries
to resolve the moral paradox by turning everything in the
nonhuman world into an object, to be utilized as we
wish. But once we disenchant the rivers, forests, soil, and
air, we end up destroying the network of life upon which
we depend.

The proper task of religion is to remind us that, in
spite of the tragic aspect of life that must feed on other
life in order to survive, we should tread reverently on the
earth and be compassionate to all sentient beings. We
may not be able to speak convincingly about the transcendent God of traditional religion or of a kingdom of
heaven beyond history, but we are not left without wit-
nesses to the sacred. The Logos, the Word, the Divine
Hologram that informs the cosmos—all things great and
small—is still spoken in sparrow song, wind sigh, and
leaf fall. An electron is a single letter, an atom a complex
word, a molecule a sentence, and a mockingbird an entire epistle in the great ongoing saga. The ocean still
whispers the song that originated with the big bang. Listen to the longing in your heart for love and justice, and
you may hear the sacred word. To live in a reverential
manner is not to surrender to authority, scripture, or institution but to create an autobiography in which we tell
the stories of the unique epiphanies that have informed
our lives.

No-thing
in the world
is sacred.
Every-thing is:
wonderful, not miraculous,
awe-full, not lawless,
graceful, not capricious,
sacramental, not supernatural,
abounding in epiphanies,
lacking any final revelation
of a divine purpose or plan.

EXPLORING THE PRIMAL UNCONSCIOUS

In 1987, when I began the search for a source of water for the house I planned to build, the rains had long since come and gone, leaving Agua Caliente a parched creek bed in the pitiless August sun. In the low, shaded parts of the watershed, tall clumps of grass marked the last shallow pockets of moisture. As I climbed through tangled tree-fall and poison oak, I noticed a small stand of verdant ferns growing above the streambed, alongside a rock as big as a barn. Pushing my hands into the dirt I could feel the moisture. What was its source?

Using a sharp stone I began to dig until the seep of

water disappeared beneath the rock. In the days that followed I used pick and shovel to clear a basin under the massive rock. When the muddy water settled, I saw two small, clear streamlets flowing from somewhere farther beneath it. Over the course of the next month I fashioned a spring box out of concrete blocks and redwood planks, keeping a careful watch on the outflow—a steady four gallons of crystal-clear water per minute. When the rains returned and the creek was swollen, I knew for certain that my spring would not be affected by the seasons. It came from occult water moving far beneath the surface of the land. Its ultimate source? Unknown.

. . .

To thrive in the desert, the sojourner must learn to explore and dig to find reliable sources of water, a small spring or an oasis that remains green in dry times. Learn the ancient art of divining. Become a skilled dowser, sensitive to the slightest vibrations of hidden streams moving like doodlebugs beneath the sands, able to detect even a faint trace of moisture in the air and any slight hint of green in the parched landscape.

The central thesis of this book is that the elemental emotions—wonder, terror, anxiety, fascination, gratitude, joy, compassion, humility, reverence, and the feeling of absolute dependency (all of which we will examine in

some depth)—are innate responses to the human condition that spring from a source deeper than the culturally
informed psyche. Unfortunately, they have been sent
into exile in the primal unconscious by a culture that
honors the secular virtues of possession, consumption,
competition, and technological innovation more than
the sacred virtues of wonder, reverence, gratitude, compassion, et cetera. Currently, these elemental emotions
are a birthright, a treasure, waiting to be reclaimed. It is
by recalling them from their exile and bringing them
into the light of consciousness that we may recover the
art of living in a sacred landscape.

Sigmund Freud taught us that we systematically repress
memories of our private hells, where we were tortured by
shame, guilt, fear, anxiety, isolation, and loneliness, as well
as memories of innocent pleasures of the senses and over-
flowing erotic energy. But because of his antireligious bias,
Freud failed to see that we also repress memories of times
when we were at harmony with the sacred. In his hostility
to anything mystical or occult, Freud was very much a
product of his age. He took great pride in the prevailing
scientific myth of his time—that the world is a mechanism
in which the human observer is separate from the observed
object. The result was detachment from our ecstatic
union with nature, which led, in turn, to the end of enchantment.

Every culture creates its own unique unconscious that

reflects what is prized, what is taboo, and what is not even imagined. What we forget or ignore is the flip side of what we choose to pay attention to and value. What is repressed in one age is overt in another. Freud undertook a courageous raid on the unconscious of his time. Currently, every vice or moral perversion that was sequestered in his account of the Victorian unconscious is paraded on MTV, celebrated on Wall Street, or flaunted on the Internet. In the unbridled twenty-first century, lust, gluttony, greed, sloth, wrath, envy, and pride, if not exactly virtues, have moved from the unconscious to the center stage of prime-time television.

The elemental emotions we repress stand in stark contrast to psychological emotions, such as shame, guilt, envy, pride, patriotism, and honor, which make up a palette of responses provided by culture. What we call our ego, or psyche, is informed by stories, myths, ideologies, and emotions we have absorbed from our parents, our peers, and our surroundings.

For instance, our basic instinct for self-preservation will trigger the impulse to flee or fight when we encounter a threatening situation. But it is from our tribal upbringing, not our hardwired instincts, that we learn the dark habit of dehumanizing our enemies that is necessary for conducting war. Children may spontaneously squabble when they do not get what they want, but they are not innately hostile. But good Serbs and Tutsis can be systematically conditioned to fear, hate, and slaughter good Croats and Hutus without the slightest remorse.

The competitive impulse that is a source of pride for an American businessperson will feel shameful to an Australian aboriginal. Clearly, a consumer society depends for its existence on the stimulation of insecurity and envy. Without a Rolex and a BMW you are not living up to your full potential. Advertising creates desire, lust to possess what our neighbors possess. We covet their lifestyle, unaware that they may be suffering from affluenza or overwhelmed by credit card debt.

When the elemental emotions are shrouded or repressed, we cease to experience the sublime nature of all life and we begin to respond to our environment in purely utilitarian ways. Our inborn sense of reverence is occluded, and the dignity of being is replaced by the frenzy of doing. We exchange our sacred birthright for a cultural myth because it promises a secure identity, a necessary role, and a sense of belonging to the tribe.

We can detect the existence of the primal unconscious by observing the emotional void in our inner lives. Where there should be a plenum of vivid emotions there is a vacuum. We diagnose depression in a similar way, by identifying the absence of joy, the repetition of destructive behavior, the lack of spontaneity, and the addiction to substances or relationships that enslave but do not satisfy.

The miracle of the human spirit is that it can always

be renewed and resurrected. Hope thrives in perpetually fertile ground. No matter how repressed, elemental emotions remain alive in the primal unconscious. Like seeds, they lie dormant in the desert for years but bloom with the first rain.

Startling Scientists, Plant Fixes Its Flawed Gene

. . . In a startling discovery, geneticists at Purdue University say they have found plants that possess a corrected version of a defective gene inherited from both their parents, as if some handy backup copy with the right version had been made in the grandparents' generation or earlier.

The finding implies that some organisms may contain a cryptic backup copy of their genome that bypasses the usual mechanisms of heredity. . . . Equally surprising, the cryptic gene appears not to be made of DNA, the standard hereditary material.

—Nicholas Wade, *New York Times,* March 23, 2005

Humans are no less resilient than plants. We have the innate capacity to create a corrected version of the defective gene (myth or meme) we inherit from our parents and our culture. At any instant our elemental emotions can waken us from our amnesia so we might cherish the incomprehensible gift of existence.

In the opening decades of a century rife with ideologically inspired conflict and chaos we need to undertake a new expedition into the interior, different from but no less daring than the one Freud took a century ago. The goal of our venture is to make a raid on the primal unconscious, to reclaim and map the elemental emotions and create what philosophers call a phenomenology of the experience of the sacred. By recovering the universal and timeless sense of living in a sacred cosmos, we may be able to grow beyond the scourge of religious warfare, or the seduction of secular salvation through science and technology, and find the common ground that binds us in a single community.

4

Remembering Elemental Emotions

How could I have expected that after a long life I would understand no more than to wake up at night and to repeat: strange, strange, strange.... O how funny and strange.

—CZESLAW MILOSZ

This primary intuition of the strangeness of it all, of our single selves as unspeakably fragile and brilliant observers of a grandeur for which we have tried through all our generations to find words, this is the experience that seems to me to underlie religion.

—MARILYNNE ROBINSON, "CREDO," *HARVARD DIVINITY BULLETIN*, SPRING 2008

At long last, we arrive at the center of the oasis, where springs bubble up from unknown depths and the shade of many palm trees protects us from the noonday

sun. Here our treasure—primordial emotions long sequestered in the primal unconsciousness—is reclaimed,
and we are fully initiated into the abiding presence of the
sacred in our ordinary/mysterious world.

To begin with, we might visualize the elementary emotions as a ring of ancient stones, each of which we must
touch in order to gain the wisdom we need to be fully initiated into the sacred perspective. But this image is too
static to do justice to the dynamic interrelations between
the emotions. Although we make distinctions between elemental emotions, they are, in fact, inseparable. They flow
into and out of one another, endlessly. One makes sense
only in relation to the others. We cannot exile any one elemental emotion from consciousness without diminishing
them all. Our basic choice is either to open ourselves to the
full range of emotions or to limit ourselves to a monochro-
matic life. By trying to avoid emotions such as anxiety,
dread, and grief, we fall into a shallow, forced optimism in
a doomed effort to remain on the sunny side of life.

Imagine, instead, looking into a kaleidoscope with the
full color spectrum. The first pattern you see might be
mostly red, surrounded by a blue halo. Give the kaleidoscope a twist, and now you see largely yellow, with overtones of green and undertones of black. Every twist leads
to a new pattern, a new emphasis, but no matter how
many times you turn the kaleidoscope you never achieve
a pattern that does not contain all of the colors.

WONDER/AWE

The sense of wonder
that is our sixth sense.
And it is the natural religious sense.

—D. H. LAWRENCE

Wonder is the alpha and the omega of the human mind. It stands at the beginning and end of our quest to understand ourselves and the world. Aristotle said philosophy begins in wonder. It is the most primal of emotions, at once ordinary and disturbing. As the sixth sense, the natural religious sense, wonder is the royal road that leads us to the other elemental emotions, and thus to a renewed sense of the sacred.

The emotion of wonder is elicited over and over again by the startling realization that there is no reason for the world or anything in it to exist, myself included. On any mouse-gray ordinary day, our sense of comfort may suddenly disappear and be replaced by the troubling awareness that it is passing strange that anything exists. As our quotidian certainties vanish we are troubled by the most basic of all the unanswerable questions that have haunted humankind. Why? Why this multitude of entities—hummingbirds, pine trees, and fish in the sea? Where did it all come from? When? Why?

When I am wonder-struck, my ordinary self-confidence vanishes, and I am rattled by the realization that I cannot understand the bare fact of my own existence. No matter how much self-knowledge and wisdom I acquire, I am, and will remain, a mystery to myself.

The experience of wonder sweeps the ground from under our feet because it sweeps aside all explanations. Nevertheless, theologians and scientists alike continue to practice their metaphysical high jumps and busy themselves creating answers to the ultimate "why" question. Masters of linguistic sleight of hand, they can make it appear, from time to time, that they have discovered an explanation.

Theologians insist that the existence of the world demands a source beyond itself: the world exists because God created the heavens and the earth! (But then who created God?)

Scientists posit no God but assume everything can be explained by the physical laws of nature, beginning with the big bang. (But what was before the beginning, before time and space came into being?) However, it turns out that the laws of nature are no more capable of explaining the universe than is a transcendent God. Ludwig Wittgenstein put it this way: "The whole modern conception of the world is founded on the illusion that the so-called laws of nature are the explanations of natural phenomena. . . . Thus people today stop at the laws of nature, treating them as something inviolable, just as God and Fate were treated in past ages."

No explanation satisfies us for long. All metaphysical and theological explanations scratch the itch in the mind for a moment but eventually only make it worse. No matter how frequently we awaken to the irreducible mystery of being, it is always a rude awakening. We are shocked, surprised, and reduced to silence. Evidently, we are not placed in this world to understand it. To wonder is, for a brief moment, to remember that we have forgotten the miracle of bare existence.

In his classic book *The Idea of the Holy*, Rudolf Otto describes the encounter with the world in a sacred manner as an experience composed of three elements—mystery, fascination, and awe-terror. We perceive the mystery of existence as at once awesome-terrifying-majestic-overpowering and fascinating-wonderful-promising-desirable. In the same measure that we shudder and recoil from the raw power of Being, we are drawn to the infinite source of beauty, nurturance, and creativity from which we have emerged and which sustains us in life.

To attain some clarity about the complex weave of elemental emotions, we need to distinguish between these two strands of experience that make up the braid of wondering awareness. But in fact these strands are so intertwined as to be inseparable. Living as we do in the neighborhood of both terror and enchantment, we experience our days marked by ambivalence and paradoxical feelings.

Whether wonder is triggered by a glimpse of a radiant sunflower, the placid face of a sleeping child, or the dreadful sound of a dying man's last breath, it throws us off stride. The world experienced as a holy mystery is always terrifying and enchanting. This eternally changing universe and this finite self that bears my name are both alive and dying—vitality and decay locked in an endless embrace.

Last week an anonymous technological messenger delivered to my e-mail address a video journey into the immensity of the macrocosm and the minuteness of the microcosm. "The Powers of Ten" began with a photo of leaves in a garden and proceeded to expand the focus by factors of 10—from leaf to forest to town to Florida to Earth to the solar system, until at the power of 10 to the 23rd power, we arrive somewhere beyond the galaxies in the darkness of space. The focus of the camera then turned back to the leaves with which we began our journey and took us on a microcosmic journey this time, shrinking our perspective by factors of ten—from leaf to cell to nucleus to chromosome to DNA chain to cloud of electrons, until, at 10 to the 16th power, we ended in an imagined patch of quarks.

Watching the video, I felt as if I was standing beside

Pascal, engulfed in the infinite spaces. "Terrified and astounded, to be here not there. . . . The memory of a guest that tarried for a day."

Faced with the raw destructive power of a hurricane or a raging flood, we feel threatened rather than delighted, impotent rather than blessed. Small boats in a typhoon-tossed sea. Like grasses of the field, we are passed over by the wind and we are gone. In the vastness of time and space our individual lives are passing clouds. To be human is to be overwhelmed—and to tremble with awe.

Our position on this third planet from the sun gives us reason to feel both gratitude and terror, both graced by the luxurious ecosphere that is our home and abandoned by the fickle powers that created us. Bertrand Russell eloquently gave voice to the awful loneliness that haunts the human condition. "Brief and powerless is man's life; on him and all his race the slow, sure doom falls pitiless and dark. Blind to good and evil, reckless of destruction, omnipotent matter rolls on its relentless way." This leaves man with the sole option to remain "proudly defiant, . . . to sustain alone, a weary but unyielding Atlas, the world that his own ideals have fashioned despite the trampling march of unconscious power."

Yet how can we not feel graced to inhabit the only place in the known cosmos where complex life—from indigo buntings to dolphins—has come into being? Here alone in all the vastness, spirit became incarnate in flora, fish, fowl, reptile, and mammal. So far, even our most advanced astronomical probes have found no celestial real estate nearly as promising as a Nevada desert. We are privileged to inhabit a planet where some incomprehensible intelligence prepared the conditions necessary for our emergence and prosperity. Through no virtue of our own, we have been ordained kings and queens of the unique kingdom of Earth.

Hiking down the old hermit trail into the Grand Canyon on an October afternoon, I watch the sun cast my minuscule shadow onto the face of a cliff a thousand feet tall, untold millions of years old. As I descend out of the direct sunlight, my shadow disappears into the deepening dusk. I am simultaneously struck by the awesome majesty of the eternal red rock and by a sense of my own insignificance in the scheme of things. How quickly I lose my place in the sun.

> The larger the island of knowledge, the longer the
> shoreline of wonder.
>
> —Ralph Sockman

GRATITUDE

You can feel either grateful or alienated, but never both at the same time. Gratefulness drives out alienation;

there is not room for both in the same heart. When you are grateful you know that you belong to a network of give-and-take and you say, "yes" to that belonging. This "yes" is the essence of love.

—Brother David Steindl-Rast

Through gratitude we perceive existence as an unconditional gift, a blessing, a beatitude bestowed on us that we have neither earned nor deserved. No matter that sometimes we suffer, struggle, and eventually will cease to exist. Nothing can destroy the gratitude we feel in this timeless moment for the privilege of being within the eternal mystery of Being.

Gratitude, joy's twin, is the antidote to the poisonous resentment that springs from a sense of entitlement. It can heal the bitterness that creeps into intimate relationships when one or both partners feel they have not received the unconditional love that is their due. It is equally curative for consumers who "wanted it all and wanted it now" but have been disillusioned by finding that they can never get enough to satisfy their desires. The simple alchemy that converts bitter to sweet converts our habitual attitude from "I demand" to "Thank you."

In his autobiography, Vladimir Nabokov describes the

gratitude he feels in the presence of a rare butterfly. "This is ecstasy, and behind ecstasy is something else, which is hard to explain. It is like a momentary vacuum into which rushes all that I love. A sense of oneness with sun and stone. A thrill of gratitude to whom it may concern—to the contrapuntal genius of human fate or to tender ghosts humoring a lucky mortal."

For those with an inclination toward religion, gratitude is expressed as praise to G-d from Whom All Blessings Flow. But there is no need to make a leap of faith to a transcendent creator who is responsible for our existence. Gratitude may lead to worship or it may remain a simple acknowledgment that our existence is an inexplicable gift.

I stop to visit my old friend Huston Smith in his new apartment in an assisted-living facility. He is working at the computer when I arrive, his hearing aids disconnected. Seeing me, he explodes with delight, and opens his arms wide in welcome. To my inquiries about his health he replies, "I have a friend who told me that getting old is nothing but pure hell. I see what he means, but it isn't like that for me. I can lay claim to one virtue—gratitude."

> If the only prayer you said in your whole life was "thank you," that would be sufficient.
>
> —MEISTER ECKHART

ANXIETY/DREAD

A year ago, while in Iran, I fell and struck my head on a stone ledge. Bloody and dazed, I was taken to one hospital after another until we found one with a CAT scanner. My scalp wound was sewed up, and I was pronounced fit to travel back to the United States. Three weeks later, I developed a hematoma and underwent three brain surgeries. In the months of slow recovery that followed, I had ample opportunity to meditate on the nature of existential anxiety. Not necessarily with a tranquil mind! Now, fully recovered, I appreciate how the experience stripped me of my illusions of invulnerability and left me with an abiding sense of anxiety. But also with lingering gratitude for the care and love I received and a vivid appreciation of daily mysteries and fleeting beauties.

I exist, therefore I am anxious. Vastness destroys my comfortable illusion that the world ever can provide me a secure home. Once shocked into awareness, I am infected by the knowledge that my existence is perpetually threatened.

The existentialists, beginning with Pascal and Kierkegaard, remind us of the elemental emotions connected to the threatening nature of existence. Against all claims of bright-eyed optimists—from Hegel to the modern prophets of technological progress—the existentialists declared that it was the perennial human condition to stand anxiously on a narrow promontory surrounded by nothingness. We are thrown into a world we can never understand, certain of the advent of our death but uncertain of its date, freighted with the need to forge a reason for living. The shock of finitude leaves us vulnerable to despair.

Existential anxiety and dread, far from being neurotic emotions that should be treated with tranquilizers, reveal our true metaphysical state. The burden they impose on us is inseparable from our awareness of our responsibility for our actions, decisions, and choices. Walt Whitman claims he wants to "turn and live with animals, they are so placid and self-contained . . . They do not sweat and whine about their condition." But I doubt he would have sacrificed the self-awareness, anxiety, and creativity without which he would not have been Walt Whitman. Anxiety met with courage is the mark of human dignity. I believe it may be otherwise for the squirrels that spend their days blissfully obsessed with the problem of how to raid my bird feeder.

Give the kaleidoscope a quarter turn, the colors change; figure and ground shift. In an instant anxiety gives way to courage and joy.

JOY

We are surprised by joy for the same reason we are assaulted by anxiety. Unaccountably, incredibly, the world into which we have emerged is endlessly fascinating. There is no reason why we should be presented with all these fleeting marvels—an orchid, a ripe peach, a child who carries my genes forward into an unknown future. Incursions of joy are constant reminders that we dwell in a portentous universe that will sometimes break our hearts and sometimes delight us.

I was driving down Route 1, the Pacific Coast Highway, to Big Sur when I came upon a sign warning ROAD WORK AHEAD. A flagman wearing a four-day growth of beard, muddy Carhartt overalls, and a hard hat signaled me to stop and ambled toward my car. As I opened the window, he leaned down and without preliminaries blurted out, "What does it mean? What does this mean?" "What does *what* mean?" I asked. Pushing the cell phone in his hand at me, he said, "I just got a call from my daughter, and she's pregnant! What does this mean?" As if discovering something miraculous, he continued: "It means I'm going to be a grandfather. I'm going to have grandchildren."

Joy just happens. No rhyme, no reason. At any moment the world surrounding us can change from black-and-white to Technicolor. An unaccountable happiness, not necessarily related to anything important, might steal upon us. It might be triggered by something as simple as a smile from a stranger or the momentary awareness that an oatmeal cookie and a cup of tea exactly fulfills the heart's desire on a cold afternoon, or the discovery that one is becoming a grandfather.

Or it might be, as the philosopher Ernest Becker told me on his deathbed, that joy bursts forth after a long, dark night of the soul when the suffering of life is not overcome but accepted. "The sense of joy is something achieved after much tribulation, where . . . all activity stops to listen to a bird. . . . At the very highest point of faith, there is joy because one understands that it is God's world and since everything is in His hands, what right have we to be sad—the sin of sadness. But it is very hard to live that."

GRIEF/MOURNING

Blessed are those who mourn, for they shall be
comforted.

—MATTHEW 5:4

Mourning is an elemental emotion elicited by confronting what Carl Jung called "the terrible ambiguity of immediate experience." How could we possibly gaze clear-eyed at the horror of Chronos eating his children, Kali destroying her creation, the Lord God giving life with one hand and remorselessly dealing death with the other? No doubt, from an Olympian perspective, this is as it should be. But I cannot so easily see the benevolence of dying when it concerns me and mine. The stage on which my life plays out was once filled with the vivid presence of marvelous actors whom I have loved. Now it is crowded with ghosts. There are no rainbows without blues.

REVERENCE

Gratitude bestows reverence, allowing us to encounter everyday epiphanies, those transcendent moments of awe that change forever how we experience life and the world.

—JOHN MILTON

Reverence—the feeling of being in the presence of someone, something, or some place we experience as sacred—may be elicited by a meadow carpeted with a profusion of royal-blue lupines, a herd of thousands of wildebeests migrating in the Serengeti, an ancient image of

Avalokitsvara, the compassionate god of a thousand hands and eyes, an icon of Christ in a cathedral, or a two-year-old child laughing on a jungle gym. Reverence induces a desire to speak in a hushed voice, to walk softly on the earth, to kneel and give thanks for the privilege of being. There is something about walking in a grove of ancient redwoods that reduces us to silence.

The feeling of reverence need not be connected to a belief in God, but institutional religion at its best creates rituals, stories of saints, places of worship, and scriptures to remind believers to practice reverence, gratitude, and compassion. Prophetic religion guards against the tendency of church and state to misplace reverence. By continually renewing our sense of wonder and reverence, we eliminate the need for allegiance to the idols of false piety, tribal morality, and creedal orthodoxy.

It is possible to imagine that in some distant future the great world religions might disappear. And it is difficult to predict whether such an event would be disastrous or benevolent. What is certain is that should our elemental instinct for reverence be lost we would be left with no defense against narcissism, nihilism, and anarchy. Reverence is what puts the "civil" in "civilization." It lies at the heart of all ethics.

It was not until he went to Africa as a medical missionary that Albert Schweitzer was able to formulate his philosophy of life, despite having studied theology for decades in the best universities in Germany. One evening at sunset, while traversing a river populated by a herd of hippopotamuses, he had an epiphany. He coined the phrase "reverence for life," which became his single rule for conduct. "By having a reverence for life, we enter into a spiritual relation with the world . . . we become good, deep, and alive."

EMPOWERMENT

One of the charges that thinkers such as Nietzsche and Bertrand Russell have leveled against religion is that it is a crutch for those who are too weak to face the indifference of the cosmos and confront the wintry smile of truth. It is an opiate of the people, okay for little old ladies and timid souls, but not for the manly.

Years ago, following the death of my father, I felt impotent and empty. One day, sitting in a church, I randomly opened a hymnal and my eyes fell on the words "When we are strong, Lord leave us not alone our refuge be." I felt in such desperate need of a power source beyond myself—God the Father—that I could not imagine why I would need God if I felt strong.

In subsequent years, my understanding of power and impotence has changed. I now believe that, contrary to popular opinion, religion in the raw draws more from an experience of power than from weakness. Certainly, when we first awaken to the sacred nature of our existence we are assaulted by our profound insignificance. We are but dust and ashes. We are impermanent and without the power to will our own existence. The primal human condition is the result of a one-party contract imposed on us by whatever power has brought us into being.

Paradoxically, it is within this experience of transience and absolute dependency that a unique sense of personal potency is born. Ernest Becker, the prominent psychoanalytic anthropologist, put it this way: "The human animal has no strength, and this inability to stand on one's own feet is one of the most tragic aspects of life. When you finally break through your character armor and discover your vulnerability, it becomes impossible to live without massive anxiety unless you find a new power source. And this is where the idea of God comes in. At its best, religion reveals both truths about man: his worm likeness as well as his godlikeness. Religious heroism involves living in primary awe at the miracle of the created object—including oneself in one's own godlikeness."

I am no-thing and everything, an impotent part of an omnipotent whole, a sinner (sundered) and a saint (whole).

How does the vision of the sacred become the ultimate power source in the life of a believer?

The profane vision sees power as happenstance—faceless, impersonal, and blind. The essence of power is the coercive force, or impact, one mindless entity exerts on another. Nature is a theater of raw power, "red in tooth and claw" (Tennyson, Darwin), in which only the fittest survive. Society is "a condition of war of everyone against everyone" (Hobbes). Politics is nothing but a game of amoral power (Machiavelli or Henry Kissinger).

From the perspective of the sacred vision, the profane notion of power makes no sense because there are no separate entities, no disconnected facts. To speak of "G-d"—the code word for the original systems theory—is to assert that all reality is intercourse, interconnection, and interaction. The starting point for any religious philosophy is a metaphysical vision of communion. The many are encompassed in one universe. Subtract interaction and there would be neither G-d, nor cosmos, nor human beings.

Religion in its original sense is the yoke that binds us in a celebration of our inter-being. The communion of believers is rooted in the awareness that to be alive is to partake of the divine power. The body of G-d is our daily bread. Sacred potency is rooted in an experience of the essential Self and the world as manifestations of the power of Being. As Joseph Campbell said, "All things and beings . . . are the effects of a ubiquitous power . . . known to science as energy, to the Melanesians as *mana*, to the

Sioux Indians as *wakonda,* the Hindus as *shakti,* and the Christians as the power of God."

This experience of residing within the empowering creativity of a sacred cosmos brings the best of religion into line with modern science in rejecting old notions of mechanistic power. Science, cybernetics, ecology, and religion are all moving beyond the vision of a universe made up of separate entities interacting by chance and mechanical causality.

The Newtonian model of power works well where there is a clear distinction between here and there, now and then, Self and Other. But it breaks down when we enter a quantum universe where entities are at once particles that exist in some local, temporal region of the multiverse and timeless waves of surging energy that bind the many into a single universe. Using metaphors borrowed from quantum physics helps us make sense of the mystical experience of empowerment and the identity of Self and Other.

> In principle, all metaphors derived from a physical world of impacts, forces, energy, etc., are unacceptable in explanations of events and processes in the biological world of information, purpose, context, organization and meaning. The "power" metaphor . . . must be looked at, as a functioning falsehood or error, causing pathologies.
>
> —GREGORY BATESON

Here is a rough map showing the topography of the competing notions of power, energy, and human consciousness:

Profane power is:	*Sacred energy is:*
mechanistic	purposeful
coercive	alluring
forceful	erotic
speedy (chronological)	patient (kairotic)
diminished by being shared	increased by being shared
divisive	uniting
competitive	cooperative

Mystics and radical explorers in every religious tradition describe an epiphany that took place when they passed through the looking glass and realized that the Self was animated by the same energy that animates the cosmos. The spotlight of consciousness that has always been anxiously searching for God turns toward the Self only to realize, as Saint Augustine said, that "what we are looking for is what we are looking with." To use a metaphor from quantum physics, my spirit is to the encompassing Spirit as a particle is to a wave (spirit : Spirit :: particle : wave).

Since we exist within the reality for which we have been searching, the spiritual imperative leads us down into the primal unconscious, into the ground of our awareness. It calls us to remember who we are. The imagination of the West has always been dominated by metaphors of the journey, the pilgrimage, and the road. We have always been a people on the move, going beyond the horizon toward a better future. What if there is no place to go? No hidden G-d to be found at the end of the quest?

> Be still.
> Stop, look, listen.
> Descend.
> Look to your roots.
> Remain radical.
> Touch the quick.

> It will not come by watching for it. It will not be said, "Look, here!" or "Look, there!" Rather, the Father's kingdom is spread out upon the earth, and people don't see it.
>
> —GOSPEL OF THOMAS

POTENTIALITY/PURPOSE/VOCATION

The awareness of having a vocation, of being summoned for some purpose, is connected to the experience of gratitude and sacred potency.

At the heart of self-awareness is the realization that I am not a standardized unit that can be replaced by another standardized unit. I am not a specimen, or a member of a species that evolved from a chance collision of particles in the cosmic soup. The state may consider me a citizen to be numbered, taxed, conscripted, and fitted into a five-year plan. My employer may consider me a resource to be used or discarded. But I fit into no pigeonhole. I am a bud beginning to unfold on a cosmic tree.

The life given me is a rich bundle of talents and potentialities I may choose to actualize or not. My unique and unrepeatable life is a work in progress that depends on my will, imagination, and energy to bring it to fruition. As I struggle to actualize my gifts, to respond to my vocation, I am empowered to experience the fullness of being. As the Gospel of Thomas has Jesus saying, "If you bring forth what is within you, what you have will save you."

The sense of purpose involves the conviction that my most idiosyncratic gifts are an integral part of the divine creative process—the eighth day of creation. Ernest Becker expressed the thought most poignantly on his deathbed. "What makes dying easier is . . . to know that beyond the absurdity of one's own life, beyond the human viewpoint, beyond what is happening to us, there is the fact of tremendous creative energies of the cosmos that are using us for some purpose we don't know. To be used for divine purposes, however we may be misused, that is the thing that consoles."

From within the experience of the sacred, I understand that the words *power, potential, promise, purpose,* and *vocation* are identical.

Power comes from the Latin *potentia*—potential.

My potential is discovered in the unfolding of my talents and gifts.

My power increases as I fulfill the promise of my being.

My vocation is the voice of my future beckoning.

My gifts, my vocation, are woven into my DNA.

My end (telos) is in my beginning.

My DNA is a strand in the ongoing process of creation.

The power-potential-promise of my being is integral to Being-Becoming-Itself.

We pop into existence without having been provided with an owner's manual and must create a sense of meaning for our individual lives. For some, this absence of intrinsic purpose creates massive anxiety. The existentialist Jean-Paul Sartre said the fact of existence was nauseating, more burden than gift—and we were "condemned to be free."

My gratitude for existence brings with it a vague sense of obligation and some puzzling questions. How, to whom or what, do I express my gratitude for this privilege? To what address do I send my thank-you card?

What am I to do with my allotted years and restless energy? What is the purpose of my life?

But there is a twist that suggests a specific path for some individuals. Of extraordinary people we frequently say they are "gifted." It was obvious from earliest childhood that Bach had a musical gift, Georgia O'Keeffe a gift for painting, and Einstein a gift for theory. Lesser mortals usually go through a long process of trial and error before they discover their gift for cooking, teaching, parenting, or governing. Whether I become aware that I am exceptionally gifted or have more modest gifts and talents, I feel an obligation to actualize that potential. (*Obligation,* from the Latin *obligare,* from *ob,* "toward," + *ligare,* "to bind." Note: It has the same root as *religion.*)

Something calls, beckons me. The voice is insistent and indistinct. I can't make out the words or specific commands, but I have a strong sense that I am being summoned. By whom? Or what? The voice comes to me like an echo reverberating from the walls of a remote canyon. The call of vocation seems to issue from the future rather than the past. It encourages me to be and to become who I am meant to be—to live up to the promise that has animated me since the beginning.

This becomes clearer when we connect the ideas of conscience, vocation, and action. My vocation is to explore and develop whatever talents, power, intellect, beauty, and strength I possess, and to share these gifts with others. The impulse to translate my gift into actions that contribute to the well-being of the community springs from gratitude and compassion.

Understandably, we have conflicting desires—to embrace and escape the voice that calls us to develop our gifts to the fullest. There is a burden that attends the sense of having a vocation. To acknowledge an obligation to develop our gifts is to be bound to a destiny that is not entirely of our own creation and to renounce the idea of absolute freedom. For many who live in affluent societies it is tempting to settle for a job that offers the normal satisfactions of status, power, wealth, entertainment, and comfort. A life without obligation escapes the burden of discovering and developing the gifts that shape our individual destiny, but it also sacrifices the joy. For even more people, the majority of the poor, who live with constant scarcity, hunger, and warfare, the constant struggle for survival leaves little energy for exploring a creative vocation.

Vocation—a voice from my future, an in-dwelling impulse that draws me forward, a love song calling me to fulfill the promise of my life.

EMPATHY/COMPASSION

When we finally know we are dying, and all other
sentient beings are dying with us, we start to have a

burning, almost heartbreaking sense of the fragility and preciousness of each moment and each being, and from this can grow a deep, clear, limitless compassion for all beings.

—SOGYAL RINPOCHE

On normal mornings, the news of the day destroys my tranquility. Yesterday, this item in the *New York Times:* "One of the most talked about stories in the Middle East last week came out of Saudi Arabia, where the government affirmed the sentence of 200 lashes for a 19-year-old Shi-ite girl who was sitting in a car with a male acquaintance last year when they were attacked by seven men who gang-raped both of them. The Saudi Justice Ministry said the young woman deserved 200 lashes and six months in prison, even though she had been raped, because she was guilty of 'illegal mingling'—sitting in a car with a man who was not related to her." In the slow hours of the night I lie awake, feel outrage, imagine the lashes falling on her back—my back.

What is this bridge joining the lone individual and the community? If I am ultimately singular, what have I to do with Thou? Why should the whip on my neighbor's back also fall on my own?

For the sake of convenience I have used the normal,

misleading shorthand in speaking about the "world" or "Being." In fact, we never come upon some entity called "world," nor do we encounter bare Being. What I call the world is not a spectacle, nor am I a spectator. When I awaken from the trance of my customary modes of thought and habitual activities—preparing my income tax or watching *Monday Night Football*—I find myself surrounded by a bewildering multiplicity of entities—the starry sky above, hawks soaring on the breeze, rats scurrying in the barn, and people of every race, color, and creed. It is precisely my illusion of singularity that is destroyed by my awareness of the plurality of beings with whom I share time and space.

Recently, neuroscientists have discovered the physiological basis for empathy and compassion. Human brains have mirror neurons that allow us to observe and mimic the actions, intentions, and emotions of others. If we watch another person dancing or being struck with a stick, our brain automatically creates a template that allows us to experience and simulate the observed action or feeling of the dancer and of the person striking and being struck. Our mirror cells automatically attune us to others at such a deep level that we feel their pain and their pleasure. It seems we are hardwired for empathy. Communion is not something added to our individuality. It is genetically given, inseparable from the human way of being in the world.

A little probing shows that the question "Who am I?" is inseparable from the question "Who is my neighbor?" Psychology, like philosophy, should begin with community rather than individuality, with "we are" rather than "I am." Wonderingly, I awaken to the realization that I am enmeshed in a web of living beings and it is only through the feeling of communion that I can understand my existence. Identity and community are inseparable. (Arguably, the malevolent groups and criminal gangs that carry out genocide and other brutal acts are also composed of individuals who mirror, identify with, and imitate others, but in this case with the perpetrators of violence rather than its victims. Something like demonic empathy seems to infect individuals who join violent groups.)

Compassion and morality flow from our existence-in-communion. Our co-familiars are, in fact, never complete strangers. From the moment of our meeting with the Other, even before we collect facts and information, we are in immediate empathic contact. Like a good therapist or novelist, we read the body, mind, and emotions of the stranger.

Wholehearted compassion emerges when we proceed from empathy to sympathy, from imagining to feeling. Our capacity for empathy and compassion allows us to understand that all living beings cherish, enjoy, and suffer their existence. All lives are wonderful, precious, and fleeting. As the Buddha said, "The first noble truth is 'existence is suffering.'" Compassion is the bond I feel with my fellow beings, my awareness of kinship. In those moments when I am moved by compassion I understand that *I* includes *Thou*. I cannot define myself narrowly in terms of self-realization, or as one half of a dyad, or a member of a nuclear family, or a patriotic citizen. I am a cosmopolitan, a member of the commonwealth of sentient beings.

But how inclusive is the commonwealth of which I am a citizen? How far can my consciousness, my compassion, my conscience, extend? Does my capacity for brotherly love include the capacity for biophilia, the love of other species of life? Who is my neighbor?

Albert Einstein spoke about how our egocentrism alienates us from other forms of life. "A human being is a part of a whole, called by us universe, a part limited in time and space. He experiences himself, his thoughts and feelings, as something separated from the rest . . . a kind of optical delusion of his consciousness. This delusion is a kind of prison for us, restricting us to our personal desires and to affection for a few persons nearest to us. Our task must be to free ourselves from this prison by widening our circle of compassion to embrace all living creatures and the whole of nature in its beauty."

I enjoy a fleeting relationship with the birds that come to my feeder (and will eat out of my hand if I am patient) and the bobcats who occasionally appear in my lower meadow. Still, I cannot imagine what it is like to be a tufted titmouse or a wild bobcat. I assume the cat possesses something analogous to my subjective awareness of myself. But there is no way I can know what it is like for a cat to be a cat. As Ludwig Wittgenstein said, "If a lion could talk, we could not understand him." We are excluded from understanding and enjoying one another's mode of consciousness. I, after all, do not eat mice or gophers, nor does my cat read the *New York Times*. Our subjective sense of self is private and impenetrable. Try as I may to imagine and empathize with cat consciousness, I cannot.

In addition, I exist within a mind-boggling commonwealth of unseen neighbors—insects, spiders, and creeping things, as well as microbes without whom I could not survive. Billions of microbes reside within every single gram of soil.

What an anomaly is Homo sapiens! Our lives are constituted and sustained by a constant intercourse between microcosms and macrocosms that remains largely beyond our understanding. Ultimately, the community within which we live and move transcends even the limits of awareness, imagination, and empathy. How strange that we, the knowing animal, are destined to remain ignorant of our myriad neighbors. Inevitably, reason sets sail into the unknown and manages to map small segments of the

shoreline before it wrecks on the shoals of the unimagin-
able diversity of living beings, leaving us awash in a sea of
wonder.

SACRED OUTRAGE

A bumper sticker on a car outside the Sonoma Market
reads, IF YOU'RE NOT OUTRAGED, YOU'RE NOT PAYING AT-
TENTION. Outrage is the other side of love, the realization
that our sacred obligation to treat others as ends rather
than means has been violated, that the compassion essential to communal life is missing.

There is a notion abroad, especially popular among
some advocates of New Age spirituality, that evil is an illusion and, therefore, that a spiritually evolved person
should be calm, accepting, and nonjudgmental. In refuta-
tion of this I offer a litany of desecration and murdered
innocents: Auschwitz, Treblinka, the gulags, the killing
fields of Cambodia, the rape of Nanking, the firebomb-
ing of Dresden and Tokyo, the nuclear holocaust in Hiroshima and Nagasaki, the genocides in Rwanda, Bosnia,
Baghdad, Darfur, suicide bombers in Israel and Manhat-
tan, the massive air strikes—Shock and Awe—in Iraq,
the routine torture of enemy combatants, the destruction
of rain forests, the pollution of the environment, the eco-

nomic exploitation of the powerless, and the crushing poverty suffered by billions.

If I can contemplate these horrors and crimes against humanity without sacred outrage, it is not because I am enlightened but because I have become morally numb. If I cannot see the shadow of evil in the bloodstained face of human history, no argument will change my mind. To wonder and revere living beings is to suffer outrage when they are desecrated. Martin Luther said love may be the proper work of God but wrath is His strange work. Even G-d must be angered by all that is destructive of love.

When living beings are reduced to abstractions, when forests become nothing but a resource to be exploited, when people become nothing but enemies to be destroyed, the elemental emotions of reverence and outrage have been abandoned. Reverence is replaced by efficiency, outrage by complacency, humility by arrogance, gratitude by greed, compassion by contempt, and cooperation by conquest. And, with this transvaluation, the sacred foundation of morality is destroyed.

HOPE

Hope is a memory of the future.

—GABRIEL MARCEL

The events of 9/11 momentarily crippled the traditional American optimism, shattered the myth of the happy ending, and plunged us into a deeply pessimistic mood. But the funerals for the terrorist victims were scarcely over when our leaders proclaimed this to be the new American century in which we would triumph over the axis of evil. Something there is in the American character that insists on being optimistic no matter what.

But optimism does not translate into hope. Optimism and pessimism are opposite poles of a continuum based on the questionable assumption that we can foresee the future. Optimists are compulsive cheerleaders, always insisting that every dark cloud has a silver lining. Theirs is a philosophy of cliché and positive thinking. Pessimists always expect the worst and are seldom disappointed or surprised; they are specialists in self-fulfilling prophecies.

I am, therefore, I hope. Hope and its close relative despair are not based on any claim to foresee the future, nor do they necessarily depend on external circumstances. The tide of hope may be full in the toughest of times. Witness South Africa and the hopeful witness of Nelson Mandela in the turbulent days of apartheid, or the American civil rights movement, or the surprising election of Barack Obama as president of the United States. As an elemental emotion, hope is not primarily something we feel; rather it is something we are; it is inseparable from the life force that drives us toward an unknown future.

How am I to understand the hope that is deeper than my consciousness, more primal than my free will? In some ways, hope seems to be built into the cycle of the seasons. Nature outside my window is always giving birth, maturing, dying, and being born again. Now, in parched summer, the Osage orange trees are yellowing toward fall, when they will strip naked under the autumn sky until spring seeds the earth once more. Each new year reveals the Möbius strip of time and eternity. Birth, death, and resurrection—an echo of the past, a memory of the future. Ad infinitum. Same old hopeful story.

All peoples throughout human history have witnessed the world end every winter and be reborn every spring in the rising of the blood and the flowing of the sap. This was not an idea. It was a visceral certainty, a natural sacrament—an outward and visible sign of the invisible grace that is curled within the DNA of all living things.

As we increasingly become a race of urban dwellers addicted to living within the virtual realities created by technology, this sacramental knowledge of the primal regenerative rhythms of the natural world is being lost.

Warning! Should we forget that the destiny of human beings is inseparable from the humus, we will lay waste our fragile landscapes, air sheds, and watersheds. And if the wild places and forest sanctuaries where wolves run free and the air receives its life-sustaining burden of oxygen disappear, both our planet and our hope will be in terminal peril. The more we destroy the homestead we have been given, the more we try to salvage a modicum of hope by entertaining fantastic, desperate dreams of escaping to other, yet undiscovered, green planets. It is, I believe, an illusion to invest our hope in such science-fiction dreams of space colonies that will house terrestrial refugees. This earth that buds and blossoms is our last best hope.

So much for blessed nature. Where do I fit in the cycle? The trees and flowers come, go, and come again. But what of me? My soul? My body? My spirit? What's my story? Am I an exception to the natural law of the conservation of energy? Does the Great Recycler relegate me to the cosmic junkyard? Am I an accidental consciousness, temporally inhabiting a rented body (rent due at time of death)? Am I some kind of orphan, a voyeur, an exile standing alone outside the wellspring of creation?

Hope is an elemental emotion that is inseparable from our life force. I hope because my being is becoming. I exist in the not-yet. I am drawn toward a future I can neither imagine nor anticipate. Longing and hope are prime movers of my existence. I am full of emptiness and yearning. No-thing satisfies my metaphysical restlessness. All that was past and is present does not exhaust the promise of my life. My best answer to the question "Are you Sam Keen?" is "Not yet."

What is the significance of this insatiable longing? It

may, as Sartre and Camus claim, be proof that we are absurd creatures driven by useless passions. Or it may be
that we are unfinished, still in the birth canal, suffering
from the larger birth pangs of a cosmos that is itself in the
process. As the ancient, mystical maxim states: As without, so within. And vice versa.

Because being is becoming, as any physicist will attest,
the question of human identity goes beyond anything
psychology taught us to ask. From a scientific point of
view, evolution is ongoing gestation. The history of nature is the story of never-ending birth. My autobiography
is inseparable from the eternal process, from alpha and
omega. The carbon in my body was once in a distant star.
My limbic brain is a heritage from reptiles. Whatever
holy power—Holographic Mind, G-d, or gods—animates this perpetually becoming world has long since
woven me into its mysterious intentions. The fingerprints
of the Ancient One are all over me.

That I exist within the life of the Ever-Renewing-
One-and-Many is a fact. How I exist is beyond understanding.

Creation is an unfinished symphony. And I? Every-
man? Everywoman? Hope is incarnate in our DNA. The
Whole is encoded in the Part. The eternal sound is imma-
nent in the breath. The sacred *om* reverberates throughout
the chakras, creating a sound body and mind. Flesh is a
tuning fork. Listen to your body.

If I were to allow myself the luxury of Christian language, I might say that in the life of the body every day is Good Friday and Easter. Death and resurrection are not singular events but the essence of the life force that animates us, the divine creation encrypted in our flesh. I am a-borning self in an a-borning universe. My gestation period is eternal. My end is not knowable. Therefore I hope.

TRUST

Trust:
The first blessing.
The final virtue.

In the beginning, trust is a gift bestowed on us—or not. Blessed the child who is held in loving arms, nurtured, and enjoyed during the first years of life, for that child will be undergirded by a sense of basic trust, security, and optimism. Unfortunate the child who is constrained in unwelcoming arms, roughly treated, or ignored, for that child will be insecure and mistrustful and will struggle throughout life with feelings of not belonging.

In the course of time, both the blessed and the unblessed will be expelled from the Garden and forced to make their way in a world in which power trumps kindness. Within the horizon of a Darwinian nature "red in tooth and claw," and a social order that Thomas Hobbes reported was "a condition of war of everyone against everyone," it is not safe to trust others, or to assume that benevolence is anything other than disguised self-interest. The universal struggle to survive, in which the strong destroy the weak, offers compelling evidence that we dwell in a brutish universe. Or worse yet, that we are imprisoned in an order created by a deity who is impotent to defeat the Evil Lord of This Age.

Confined as we are in parentheses of time and space, ignorant of the totality beyond our perspective, we are forced to make a decision before all the evidence is in—which it never will be. Once we have tasted the bitter truth that suffering is a universal destiny (a truth Buddha insisted was liberating), we reach the end of the legacy of innocent trust that was bestowed on us in childhood; now we must find a mature form of trust that lies on the far side of doubt and despair. The challenge is to discover a worldview that allows us to place trust in ourself and others, even though the world remains dangerous and unpredictable.

Reason alone is useless in determining what attitude we should adopt toward the ultimate meaning of our lives, what conclusions we should draw from a cosmic process that nurtures and slays, heals and harms, brings great joy and suffering. Whether the cosmic powers are malevolent or benign is an issue that cannot be settled by an objective appeal to the facts. Both bleak and rosy views are constructions based on a highly selective gathering of information. All worldviews are projections (Rorschach tests) that lead to self-fulfilling prophecies, a checkerboard on which black squares are superimposed on a white background or vice versa. The puzzling, unfathomable world we inhabit is systematically ambiguous, creating in us contradictory impulses to trust and not trust.

When choosing a worldview we should consider the manner of life it recommends, how it influences our conduct and self-image. Does it lead us to create the civic virtues—reverence, respect, kindness, and justice—without which we cannot be neighborly to one another? Does it encourage us to become trustworthy? Does it help us feel at home in this strange world?

If I adopt a malevolent worldview, my actions will be based on the maxim "Thou shall not trust." Predictably, I will end up a paranoid resident of a living hell. My body will become armored against tenderness and hope; I will dwell in a cosmos against which I must do battle. Without trust the world becomes a battlefield.

A mature disposition to trust is no blind leap of faith but a step from the solid ground of the daily experience of the sacred—wonder, gratitude, and the other elementary emotions—into the unknown, a step into a manner of life that is essentially religious. Ludwig Wittgenstein put it this way: "It strikes me that a religious belief could only be something like a passionate commitment to a frame of reference. Hence, although it's belief, it's really a way of living, or a way of assessing life."

A lifestyle anchored in an existential decision to trust the unknowable encompassing mystery involves an intention to be vulnerable and trustworthy. Far from being a kind of positive thinking or knee-jerk optimism, it identifies evil with all the forms of desecration—cruelty, warfare, poverty, environmental destruction—against which those with a vision of the sacred are passionately committed to struggle. Mature trust is militant, not passive.

At no time does the decision to trust or not trust become more agonizing than when we are facing death. Ultimately, with or without our consent, we will cross the narrow, one-way bridge over the void that leads from a world charged with grandeur and racked with pain into the Vast Unknown.

> In the end, when there is
> no thing to hold to,
> no known destination
> I must lie me down
> and trust the everlasting arms
> of an unknown G-d.

HUMILITY

Humility, that low, sweet root,
From which all heavenly virtues shoot.

—THOMAS MORE

Many years ago, when I was a young professor given to perpetual rebellion and iconoclasm, I stood accused of being arrogant. This confused me because, although I felt pride in my work and I put forward my views vigorously, my self-esteem wavered and I suffered from frequent bouts of self-doubt.

In search of a nostrum for my confusion, I went to the psychology section of the library and began pulling out books at random. Great good luck led me to Karen Horney's *Neurosis and Human Growth*. I checked the book out, took it home, and spent most of the night reading. The next morning I bought a copy and began underlining the passages that gave me some insight into the psycho-logic of my mood swings.

It was Horney's understanding of the nature of neurosis that offered me release. Neurosis, as she taught me, was a condition in which a person oscillated between feelings of superiority and feelings of inferiority. On any given day a neurotic might make arrogant judgments about others only to be haunted by feelings of worthlessness and humiliation. What the neurotic lacks is any realistic appreciation of the self. As I observed the constantly changing weather of my moods, I realized that her theory of neurosis accurately described my condition, and it occurred to me that a small measure of realism might end my painful mood swings.

A month later I went out drinking with an old friend and shared my struggle with arrogance and feelings of inferiority. After listening to my agonizing dilemma he said: "Sam, I always thought arrogance was one of your few *good* qualities." We laughed, but the incident left me with a lasting curiosity about the nature of humility. Why did he praise my arrogance? What did he know about me that I did not?

Of all the elemental emotions, none has a poorer reputation in modern times than humility. It is frequently identified with low self-esteem or confused with humiliation and shame. The poor, the meek, and the humble, much loved by Jesus, have no place in the kingdom of the affluent. In our highly competitive society the place of honor is reserved for the winner—the *Übermensch*. Number One! Like Nietzsche, we consider humility a false virtue that conceals weakness.

If we turn from mammon to religion, humility does not fare much better. A whiff of false piety clings to most religious definitions of humility. According to Saint Thomas, humility signifies lowliness or submissiveness. Saint Bernard defines it as "a virtue by which a man, knowing himself as he truly is, abases himself." It is frequently described as a quality by which a person, considering his own defects, willingly submits himself to God and to others for God's sake.

This idealization of lowliness and submissiveness rests on subliminal images that have long dominated the Western religious imagination, images of a servant kneeling before a master, a slave before a monarch, or a sinner before a transcendent God. If we accept such images as a true reflection of the human condition, we are obliged to bow our heads before our Lord. If we reject the entire trope—the model of Lord and Servant—we must either rebel against the divine tyrant (and be accused of arrogance by true believers) or search for a new way of thinking about G-d that identifies humility with the realization of the full promise of being human.

Refusing to abase one's self before a righteous God is not arrogance but healthy pride. It was, I believe, a measure of that pride hiding under the mask of rebellion that my friend recognized in me when as yet I could not recognize it myself.

But before we jettison the venerable idea of humility we should look at it from different perspectives.

The Buddhist approach to humility, like that of Karen Horney, is psychological. Since Buddhism does not begin by positing the existence of a transcendent God, it considers humility a virtue that must be won through a long process of self-observation. It requires a healthy measure of self-confidence and courage to achieve a realistic and humble understanding of the self. When we dare to embrace silence, solitude, and meditation, we can't help noticing that our feelings oscillate between the extremes of grandiosity and debasement. We think either too much or too little of the self. To be enlightened we must reject both extremes. As the seventh Dalai Lama said, "Who has magnificent self-confidence and fears nothing that exists? The man who has attained truth and lives free of error."

Humility is a strange, perpetually receding virtue. If you search for it, it vanishes. If you examine yourself and find you possess it, it turns into its opposite—pride or arrogance. You may observe it in a beautiful stranger or friend so long as you remain silent and say nothing about it.

Perhaps the virtue of humility is no virtue at all but only a mirror in which, by the light of the other virtues, we may see our true nature. In the neurotic Hall of

Mirrors, one mirror makes us too small and another makes us too large. It is only the mirror of humility that reflects our true size and condition. Think of humility as a diamond whose many facets mirror the elemental emotions that make up the sacred vision.

The lone diamond—humility—is surrounded by a cluster of other jewels—elemental emotions that offer a glimpse of the sacred.

> In the blinding light of wonder we discover ourselves
>   within a mystery beyond explanation.
> In the warm glow of gratitude we receive our life as a
>   gift from a source beyond ourselves.
> In awe we tremble before the overwhelming creative-
>   destructive power of the cosmos.
> In joy we are surprised by unconditional grace.
> In grief we weep for all fleeting beauty.
> In reverence we listen respectfully to the myriad voices
>   of the commonwealth of sentient beings.
> In compassion we are joined to our neighbor's sorrow
>   and joy.
> In outrage we resist the desecration of war, poverty,
>   and the pollution of streams and atmosphere.
> In anxiety and dread we feel lost in infinite space and
>   time.
> In being empowered we find ourselves infused by the
>   informing energy of the cosmos—enthusiastic.

In the echo of vocation we discover our promise and
potential.

In hope we are moved toward a fulfillment we cannot
imagine.

In trust we surrender to the unknown source of the
known world.

In humility we know our destiny is earthy—from dust
to dust—and we rest content in the luminous
darkness.

For two decades, as an editor for *Psychology Today,* I in-
terviewed all manner of psychologists, philosophers,
and gurus. Among the extraordinary individuals I was
privileged to talk with, none was more winsome and
compelling than Guru Bawa. Bawa was an ageless Sufi
mystic—at one moment he might look 14 and the next
114—who had appeared from somewhere in Sri Lanka
and established a fellowship group in Philadelphia. His
discourses were filled with parables, fun, and sage advice
to his followers. Often, without notice, he would break
into ecstatic chants in Tamil—sacred, poetic rap. He
was, to the best of my understanding, an exemplar of
humility.

"You have got to understand. In the world there is no
one as lowly as myself, and no one as roguish as myself. I
am a small man. I am a good man also. I have no wealth
of my own. . . . It is a lowly thing that is named Guru

Bawa, but very valuable. My name is Ant Man. This is the name that is given to one after he has realized himself. In this world we have got to be very small so we can travel anywhere through all the secrets of God. . . . If we possess this kind of consciousness we can build a house for the soul in this world."

5

God Talk and Sacred Nonsense

><

There are, indeed, things that cannot be put into words.
They make themselves manifest. They are what is mystical.

—LUDWIG WITTGENSTEIN

Time to pause, climb a tall tree, look around, and re-orient ourselves. After taking leave of our familiar values and lifestyles when we started to question the idol-atrous religious and secular myths of our age, we began a solitary sojourn in the desert. Just when we were tempted to despair of finding any authentic vision of the sacred, we came upon a hidden oasis and discovered a rich trove of elemental emotions that are the birthright of all who share the human condition.

We now face the challenge of what to do with our treasure. Do we hoard it, keeping it to ourselves? Should we, like the Hindu mystic Ramana Maharshi, retreat to the Mango Cave, remain silent, and meditate on the ineffable consciousness of Oneness? Does the sacred quest end with cultivating our own gardens and dwelling within our private and incommunicable experiences?

Because we human beings are verbal and communal animals, we cannot remain wonder-struck and dumb. We need to say something. We are a species given to storytelling and philosophizing to explain our world. Ergo, it is pure folly to suppose we can avoid speaking about the ultimate context and meaning of our existence. We cannot simply be content with the private experience of elementary emotions and the great encompassing mystery. Our feelings demand expression. How are we to understand this perennial need to speak *to* G-d and *about* G-d even when what we say involves contradictions, paradoxes, and sacred nonsense? To communicate is to come back into the community. The hero must return from the inner journey to the common life of dialogue and engagement.

PRAYERS TO AN ABSENT G-D

ON PRAYER

You ask me how to pray to someone who is not.
All I know is that prayer constructs a velvet bridge
And walking it we are aloft, as on a springboard,

Above landscapes the color of ripe gold
Transformed by a magic stopping of the sun.
The bridge leads to the shore of Reversal
Where everything is just the opposite and the word *is*
Unveils a meaning we hardly envisioned.
Notice: I say we; there, every one, separately,
Feels compassion for others entangled in the flesh
And knows that if there is no other shore
They will walk that aerial bridge all the same.

—CZESLAW MILOSZ

Considered rationally, speaking *to* G-d is pure nonsense, a holdover from our childish habit of submitting complaints and requests to a powerful parent. Memo to God: Dear Almighty One, please stop the genocide in Darfur, comfort the millions in Africa who are suffering from AIDS and can't afford drugs, bless your chosen people and your holy land, grant us victory over our enemies, and protect our troops and bring them home safely . . . and help me lose ten pounds. We pray, also, for the healing of our sick relative, and give thanks for the recent addition to the family. Thy kingdom come, thy will be done.

Prayer seems to be based on the assumption that God is the nerve center of some cosmic Internet that periodically suffers from a hardware failure, or a temporary triumph of evil in a remote region of the universe. In which case, prayer is a way of getting our personal computer back online to the divine source from whom all blessings flow. Or, maybe, the Eternal CEO is simply overwhelmed by the multitasking required to keep the universe running and needs a reminder of the small concerns in our neighborhood: a nudge, a letter to our congressperson, a petition to the head of state.

If the God to whom we address our concerns is omniscient, omnipotent, and ubiquitous, then He-She-It should know our thoughts from afar. And if "there is not a word on our tongue but He knoweth it altogether" (Psalm 139), why do we pray at all? Our efforts to communicate seem redundant.

Some apologists have argued that the efficacy of prayer can be scientifically proven. Supposedly, plants that are prayed for grow faster and stronger. Some double-blind experiments are alleged to prove that patients who receive prayers heal faster than those who are left solely to the ministrations of modern medicine. Other experiments claim the opposite. To my mind the whole question of the efficacy of prayer is misguided. Like the argument between atheists and theists, the issue is not an empirical one that conceivably could be settled by experiments.

Prayer makes no sense to me. Therefore, I need to understand why on occasions I find myself doing it. I pray because I can't help myself.

Several years ago I was hiking in the Himalayas when word arrived that my longtime friend Dick Ruopp had died after an agonizing struggle with ALS, Lou Gehrig's disease. As I strung Buddhist prayer flags from a swinging bridge over a rushing river, waves of grief washed through me. I ceased to be the actor and became the one acted upon, the instrument upon which a sorrowful tune was played. When someone I love is in pain or facing a great loss, when my life changes in a nanosecond and I am left standing on the boundary between life and death, when there is nothing left to do or say, impotence and hope join hands and I address the mystery out of which I have emerged and into which I will disappear.

Of course, there is something childlike about praying to a silent G-d, but Freud taught us that a small child has a permanent home within the most sophisticated psyche. In prayer, as in psychotherapy, I recover the innocent voice that utters the primal words: I am afraid, I need you, I love you, don't abandon me, I hurt, I'm sad, I don't understand. Prayer is the voice that utters our deepest feelings. As such it is destined to persist.

Who speaks a prayer and to whom is it spoken? Prayer, Martin Buber said, is a dialogue between I and an eternal Thou. But this is far too simplistic. The problem with this model is that our partner in dialogue is an un-communicative G-d, the ultimate nondirective Rogerian psychotherapist who does not reveal anything about Him-Her-Its self. But the silent presence may be precisely what we require to gain self-knowledge.

I come to prayer, to therapy, or to meditation searching for the truth about myself. The shock of self-knowledge comes with the realization that what is outside me will not (and cannot) define the purpose of my life. The silent presence of the Other reminds me that my dignity as a human being lies in accepting the dreadful and wonderful gift of my freedom.

Prayer erases the boundaries between my spirit and the Unknown Encompassing G-d. It is a form of metaphysical intercourse in which I and the Other who is the ground of my being are entwined beyond the possibility of separation. What makes prayer so strange is that it seems to address a separate Other at the same time that it acknowledges that I and the Other are inseparable.

I know of no place in religious literature where this experience of the enfolded relationship between Self and the ever-present G-d is explored more lucidly than in Psalm 139. "Whither shall I go from thy Spirit? Or whither shall I flee from thy presence? If I ascent to heaven, thou art there! If I make my bed in Sheol, thou art there! For thou didst form my inward parts, thou didst knit me together in my mother's womb. I praise thee, for thou art fearful and wonderful. Wonderful are thy works! Thou knowest me right well; my frame was not hidden from thee, when I was being made in secret, intricately wrought in the depths of the earth. Thy eyes beheld my unformed substance; in thy book were written the days that were formed for me, when as yet there was none of them."

Buddhists carry the notion of prayer a step further, into the natural world. In Bhutan, multicolor prayer flags flutter in the breeze on the tops of hills overlooking villages, in mountain passes, and alongside small farms tucked into deep valleys. In auspicious places in small streams, water-powered prayer wheels turn constantly. Small nooks in the cliffs beside the trails contain mini shrines and statuettes compressed from a mix of earth and the ashes of the dead. Many times I have wakened in a village in the predawn hours and heard monks chanting, repeating the great prayer of the Lord Buddha— *"Om mani padme om"*—a reminder of the treasure of the Dharma, the Buddha, and the Community, the jewel in the heart of the lotus. When I asked about the prayer flags and wheels, a monk explained to me: We believe that the wind and the water, like human beings, should be constantly offering prayers.

Prayer is an outer and visible expression of an inner and invisible intention to inhabit and cultivate our entire soulscape, to bring our lives under the dominion of what is sacred and abiding. It is a pledge to hold in reverence what we encounter.

Love and prayer both use special gestures and liturgies to create a world of meaning—a personal microcosm. My prayers, like the words I whisper to my beloved, are for no others to hear.

Prayer and love
Metaphoric caresses
Wonderful nonsense

ON SPEAKING ABOUT G-D

The word within the word, the unheard melody, the spirit ditties of no tone. . . . Get the nothingness back into words. . . .

Transparency. To let the light not on but in or through. To look not at the text but through it; to see between the lines; to see language as lace, black on white; or white on black.

—Norman O. Brown

Don't, for heaven's sake, be afraid of talking nonsense (Unsinn)! But you must pay attention to your nonsense. . . . I think I summed up my attitude to philosophy when I said: philosophy ought really to be written only as a poetic composition.

—Ludwig Wittgenstein

I find myself increasingly reluctant to utter the great and ancient name, the capitalized noun that is above all other nouns. The cat's got my tongue. In spite of my temptation to despair in the presence of evil (which I refuse to capitalize and give the status of a proper noun), I still have a wavering trust in the Whence and Whither of Everything. I find myself in an uncomfortable position of having a kind of visceral trust in a G-d about whom I can say almost nothing that makes sense to me. At least I am in good company. All of the great religious traditions caution against getting comfortable with our language about G-d. What theologians call the *via negativa* suggests we remain most faithful to the ultimate mystery when we remember that we know best what G-d is *not*.

In spite of my discomfort with any positive theology that claims to give us knowledge of the Unknowable One, I am interested in what happens to our imagination and our sense of identity when we make an effort to name the Totality within which we live and die. Søren Kierkegaard, the great Danish philosopher, reminded us that communication about G-d must be indirect, truth told on a slant. All authentic religious language is agnostic and poetic—a way of handling the untouchable, of pointing out that which is without location. The seemingly contradictory task of speaking about the unspeakable requires us to use everyday language, poetry, parable, and song in a consciously metaphorical way.

Recently, a band of militant atheists—Christopher Hitchens, Richard Dawkins, Sam Harris, et al.—have leveled justified attacks on popular religion for its childish views of God and its support for holy wars. Unfortunately, these new atheologians share a common assumption with fundamentalists that renders both views trivial. Both reduce the question of G-d to the question of whether a supernatural entity, a transcendent personal God, exists: if you believe in the existence of the Omnipotent, Omniscient Person, you qualify as a person of faith; if not, you are an atheist.

Why does a cloud of foolishness descend on otherwise intelligent believers, thinkers, and atheists when they talk about G-d? What causes them to speak like Sunday-school children arguing about the existence of Santa Claus?

For instance, rivers of ink have been wasted over the question of whether God is "personal." Neither the affirmations nor the denials of the existence of a "personal" God can stand up to a rational analysis. No description of the characteristics of a person—a finite, gendered, story-telling, biped animal—could possibly be applied to the Great Unknowable One and Many. We speak of G-d as personal because we are personal and we have only metaphors created by our time-bound, space-bound imaginations with which to reach for that ultimate reality that forever exceeds our grasp. If we choose to apply the metaphor "person" to the Ground of Being and Becoming, this provides us with a rationale for creating a language of prayer and praise, supplication and thanksgiving, with which we may address the otherwise ineffable Mystery. Whether or not G-d is personal is beside the point. What matters is this: we most easily express our anxieties and hopes when we imagine we are speaking to a personal being like ourselves.

It is not productive to linger long over the conclusions of the contemporary anti-God squad. Poetically challenged positivists, like blind art critics and music reviewers with a tin ear, are not our best guides to the landscape of the sacred. It is far more illuminating to study the poets, the storytellers, and the ardent but anguished critics of religion—Dostoyevsky, Feuerbach, and Nietzsche.

The question is not whether we shall talk about G-d, but how.

In Arthur C. Clarke's story "The Nine Billion Names of God," a group of computer experts is engaged by a Buddhist monastery in Tibet. Their assignment is to use an automatic sequencing computer to list all of the billions of possible names for God. According to the monks, when all the names have been recorded they will no longer need to be spoken and God's purpose will have been achieved and humankind and the cosmos will come to an end. As the project draws to a close, the computer specialists decide it would be wise for them to leave the monastery, even though they do not subscribe to the monks' apocalyptic myth. As they secretly make their way toward an airfield where they will be picked up and whisked back to civilization, they look up at the night sky—and realize that one by one the stars are going out.

What would happen if we stopped using the long-hallowed and familiar names? Would we lose our sense of the sacred and cease acting in reverential ways? I fancy that, if we abandoned our ancient theologies and liturgies and the light from the old stars began to fade, we would not be left in darkness. Something like the aurora borealis, a dancing light show of many colors, would move across the night sky instead. Freed from the old logospheres that encapsulated us with formula, creed, and authority, we might experience a new birth of theological creativity. Future religion might play with new metaphors and invent names that express our emerging understanding of the elegant mysteries of time, space, and matter. Instead of a God who leads his sheep beside still waters, or a Lord of Hosts reigning from on high, it might imagine a restless, ubiquitous DNA that is informing every cell, molecule, and mind. Or a universally local quantum power. Or, or, or. Metaphors without end, minds at play in the lordly-lowly-sacred-quotidian world we inhabit.

METAPHORS, MYTHS,
AND METAPHYSICAL HIGH JUMPS

A man's reach must exceed his grasp, or what's a
meta-for?

—Sandor McNab

There is a time to keep silence and a time to speak in a
new voice rich with overtones of laughter, play, poetry,
and fantasy. Nietzsche's words are prophetic for our time:
"When I saw my devil I found him serious, thorough,
profound, and solemn; it was the spirit of gravity. . . .
Come let us kill the spirit of gravity."

Everything I know about the ten thousand names for
the Nameless One can be summed up in a single haiku
(hi-cow).

> Mind milks
> the world
> for metaphor.
> Holy Cow!

Since the profundity of this small work of poetic genius has thus far escaped its few readers, I will make bold

to explain the many ways in which it may be a comfort to those of agnostic faith, a balm to soothe the conflicts between true believers, and an elixir to dissolve the arguments of militant atheologians angry because their impossibly defined God doesn't exist.

Human beings are the only bio-mythic animal. Our lives are informed both by the biological information encoded in our DNA and by the cultural information encoded in the memes, myths, and symbols with which we are indoctrinated by our parents, tribe, and nation. Thus we live both in an environment and a logoscape—a symbolic enclosure we create through the kinds of language we use.

Sooner or later we make heroic efforts at metaphysical high jumps that make use of metaphors, myths, and models in an effort to find the hidden unity that underlies the obvious plurality of everyday life. Every metaphor is a thought experiment, a mini-tale about the unlikely marriage between similarity and difference. Time creeps at its petty pace, or ambles along like a shuffling bear, or flies swift as an arrow. Money talks, is the mother's milk of politics and the root of all evil. Love is a red, red rose and a thorn in the flesh. In Chicago the fog is a small gray cat, while on the road to Mandalay the monsoon is a man-eating tiger.

Metaphors are openings in a thicket revealing a path that leads farther into the darkening wood than we can see with the naked eye. (This is a meta-metaphor, a metaphor about metaphors.) If we could know the literal truth (if there is a literal truth), we wouldn't need metaphors, only scientific formulas, and perhaps a bit of poetry to adorn the naked facts. But facts, being shy, never appear naked. And the Whole, being the Whole, is visible only in its parts. The Unknowable Totality (also known as the G-d of Ten Thousand Names) is a trickster who may be glimpsed in an infinite number of finite disguises—in a grain of sand, in a flower sprouting from a crannied wall, in the fearful symmetry of a tiger—but may be spoken of only in metaphor. The name of the G-d game is hide-and-seek.

As the moth to the flame, the mind flies to the Unnamable One to create names that flare for a moment and burn out in the fire of self-contradiction. Mystics of every age have recognized that metaphors for G-d can never be more than primitive symbols for the ultimate reality that lies beyond our ken and predication. God, as Joseph Campbell said, is a metaphor for that which transcends all levels of intellectual thought. After writing endless pages about how we may know and name God, Thomas Aquinas concluded by saying: "We remain joined to Him as to one unknown."

The way Einstein used quasi-theological language in a playful and consciously metaphoric sense gives us a clue to one way we might redeem G-d talk. Although he frequently spoke of "the Old One" and wondered whether God had any choice in the creation of the world, Einstein denied that he believed in any personal God. His casual use of "God" expressed deeply reverential feeling for the mystery and rationality of nature and for the incomprehensible fact that the world is comprehensible but does not point to a Super Entity. As he put it: "My religion consists of a humble admiration of the illimitable superior spirit who reveals himself in the slight details we are able to perceive with our frail and feeble mind."

When the working, analytical, scientific mind reaches a void beyond which it cannot go, the playful mind begins its speculation. As Einstein said, "Imagination is more important than knowledge." Where fact and measurement give out, our best guides are the poets, singers, storytellers, and philosophers who use fantasy and metaphor to play with possibilities that lie beyond the ken of rational intelligence. We need to honor the Dionysian promise that, now and then, the path of excess leads to the palace of wisdom. If the world is ever to be made safe from religious fanaticism, orthodox language must be replaced by a theology that knows how to play and laugh at itself. Buddhists have a saying about their sacred myths: "You are a fool if you believe these stories; you are a fool if you don't."

At best, all names for G-d are slippery handles on an

ungraspable reality. The right attitude toward sacral metaphors is one not of belief or disbelief but of experimentation and play. Bring the jesters, poets, singers, storytellers, and tricksters back into the sanctuary. After the desert, after silence, after asceticism, it is time for zany, preposterous, outlandish, droll, frisky language. It is time for laughter. Play with metaphors. Milk the Holy Cow.

A FESTIVAL OF NAMING

This is the open secret: the Emperor of the Cosmos is everywhere present but nowhere to be found. You are invited to a festival for renaming the Nameless One. As a thought experiment, invent several new names for G-d.

The rules of the game are few. For the time being, do not use the tried, true, and revered names from the authorized scriptures of any religion East, West, North, or South. Declare a verbal fast. Give Yahweh, Allah, and Almighty God a rest, along with Moses, Muhammad, and Jesus. All true believers would do well to take a page from the Buddhist scripture, which counsels devout Buddhists to kill the Buddha if they meet him on the road. Depend on no authority other than your own experience.

There is nothing wrong with the old names except that the forms in which the vision of the sacred and speculations about G-d are expressed need to expand and change in every generation. There is nothing sacrosanct about any of the institutional practices of religion—dogma, ritual, churches, sanctuaries, and mosques. Reinvent the forms, or lose the content.

Please, no names indicating gender! A couple of decades ago I was awakened from my dogmatic, patriarchal sleepwalk by Mary Daly's *Beyond God the Father*. She convinced me that language referring to God as He, Father, Lord, and King was a covert way of claiming and maintaining the superiority of men and the "masculine" virtues—reason, power, control—and of keeping women in the missionary position. In short, the theological Hearchy of Judaism, Christianity, and Islam was an ideological weapon in the war between the sexes. Even though it meant giving up my comfortable, self-serving claim to phallocentric superiority, I resolved to repent of my bias and cease applying gender predicates to the Creator and Sustainer of All. Imagine my surprise, when faster than I could say "I surrender" I was inundated by feminist manifestos proclaiming the She-archy—Motherhood of God, the Womb of Becoming, the Age of the Goddess, and the divinity of all things feminine. And nobody laughed or remembered that for the thousands of years when the Great Goddess ruled there was human sacrifice, slavery, blood, and cruelty enough for all.

It is high time we removed all tribal and gender politics

from theology and banished God from the war room and the bedroom. If we can't find a way to speak about G-d without smuggling in our political, ideological, and gender concerns, then it is time to be silent. Let's forget gender and get on with loving mercy and seeking justice for all creatures great and small who dwell in the Commonwealth of Sentient Beings regardless of race, color, creed, sexual orientation, number of legs, wings, or fins.

A new name should stretch our imaginations about what is ultimately the case on this giant ball of string in which we are all entangled. You may use nouns or verbs, but remember that in this constantly changing universe a noun is only a verb temporally at rest, a still photograph of a cascading stream.

There are names that issue from the head and those that spring from the heart. We need both. In creating new names for G-d remember that metaphors are lenses, hearing aids, sacred sensing devices. At issue is not whether they are true in some objective sense but whether they remind us to wonder, to be grateful, compassionate, and reverent.

Warning: Taking any single metaphor literally may be injurious to your physical, political, and spiritual health. Use sparingly. Alternate with other metaphors. Discontinue use if any of the following side effects occur: atrophy of the imagination, lack of a sense of humor, conviction of possessing The Truth, or loss of tolerance for other ways of understanding.

Try this: Write a short commentary to explain your new names. What do they help you see, remember, feel, do?

When I play with new language, I find that each new metaphor forces me to ask myself: What, exactly, do I mean when I speak about G-d? To what kind of experience am I seeking to give voice? In each case, I am forced back to some incident, to a personal epiphany that involved one of the elemental emotions. Each new name for G-d is a metaphysical story in a capsule that suggests something about the ultimate context of my existence.

For instance, if G-d is the Eternal Not Yet, my longing and hope are marks of my participation in the restless Ground of Being-Becoming. If G-d is the Hider and the Seeker, then, as Augustine said, "that with which I search is that for which I search" and my arduous quest has been a fool's errand—a man riding on an ox looking for an ox. What I searched for was never missing; my ego, that old master of illusion, tricked me into believing I was a separate entity. The joke is on me.

> Grace is regaining a sense of humor.
> Laugh and be liberated.
> A touch of madness is our best antidote to fanaticism.

Some suggestions to prime the pump:

Quantum Leaper
Particle Rancher
Wave Rider
The Universally Local Network
The Single Tree and the Wind That Moves It
The Singular Multiplicity
The God Formerly Known as the Ubiquitous One

The Great Hologrammer
The Lord of Fractals
The Cosmic DNA
Information Central
The Great In-former
Formerly known as Logos, Word, In-dwelling Divine
     Rationale

The Big Blossoming (Big Bang?)
The Alpha and Omega Helix
The Eternal Temporal Möbius Strip

The In-dwelling Aphrodisiac
The Universal Object Subject of Our Affections
The Care-ful One and Many
The End (Telos) of Every Love Story

Sympathetic Participant in All Suffering and Delight
Vulnerable Care-Giver
Formerly the God of Love—Agape, Eros, Philia,
    Libido

The Quick and Quickener
The Knower, the Known, and the Knowing
The Verb That Activates All Other Verbs
In-dwelling Spirit
Formerly Known as Holy Spirit

The Womb of Becoming
The Eternal Not Yet
The Ever-Evolving One and Many
The Beginner Without Ends
The Source and Sorcerer
The Black Hole Where Love Embraces Death
The All-Inclusive Noun and Void
The Subject That Encompasses All Predicates
The Cosmic Web Master
Universal Authority
Weaver of the Warp
Tale Spinner
Storyteller
Central Casting's Cosmic Host
Karmic Control Central

Cosmic Justice Enforcer
Point of Harmonic Convergence
The Forever-Being-Born Creator of Novelty
Formerly Creator, Sustainer,
    Transcendent-Immanent Intelligence

Just for the fun of it, launch your own theological pyramid scheme. Create three new names for G-d. Send them to three friends with the instruction that they should create three new names and send them to three friends, always keeping your name at the top of the list. By sowing three names you may reap a million or more new names for G-d.

The technique of playing with metaphors helps us avoid the naïve literalism that turns both G-d and the great pathfinders into supernatural beings. The dialogue between Christians, Jews, Muslims, and Buddhists would be more lively if we created new images and metaphors to help us understand charismatic figures such as Jesus, Moses, Muhammad, and Buddha. Instead of God and Savior: holy holograms; sacred fractals; double-sided mirrors reflecting divine-human life; shaman bringing wisdom from another dimension; tricksters sewing creative confusion; divine sand paintings done once and erased by the wind; prophets of the paradoxical kingdom that is inside/out, now/then, here/there, everywhere/nowhere;

incubator of our collective dream of a sacred community. Storytellers, parable spinners, koan masters. The silence of G-d made flesh.

> A new word is like a fresh seed sown on the ground of the discussion.
>
> —LUDWIG WITTGENSTEIN

6

Rites, Rituals, and Sacraments

Primitive religion is not believed, it is danced.

—ARTHUR DARBY NOCK

I can't remember exactly when the Special Day Candle appeared in our family. It seems to me the large green vase with the fat red candle had always been in a recess of the corner cupboard ready to be lit to celebrate a special event in the life of our family. Dad always presided over the ritual, but the candle was lit by whoever was being honored, for a birthday, a graduation, a marriage, a recovery from illness. New husbands, wives, and children were welcomed into the family by the lighting of the sacred flame.

Once, in August of 1945, the candle was lit to the accompaniment of horns and firecrackers on the day World War II ended. When our family dispersed to various corners of the world the candle was put away in a drawer and forgotten. On November 4, 1964, it was brought out once again to mark our father's death. We gathered around the flame for the last time on December 7, 2007, to mourn and celebrate Mother's life and death. By then the candle had burned down to a small stub, but it was still large enough to hold a lifetime of shared memories.

·   ·   ·

Human beings are ritual-making animals. We create personal and communal rituals and rites of passage to punctuate our time and remind us to revere our days. Just as we use playful and poetic language about G-d to express what cannot be captured in words, we use nonverbal sacraments to point to what cannot be seen. Daily mass for Catholics, prayer five times a day for Muslims, tai chi for the Chinese community, morning and evening meditation for Zen students and monks provide a visible testimony to the invisible elemental emotions that mark an encounter with the sacred. One part of the hero's return to the ordinary world is to discover a way to communicate the essentially incommunicable private vision of how everyday reality appears when seen as sacred rather than profane. The means for suggesting what cannot be shown are poetic language, symbolic gestures, rites, and sacraments.

Periodically, we hear confident predictions that religion

with its special rituals and sacraments will soon wither away and be replaced by an enlightened humanism. When we evaluate this scenario, we should remember the recent history of communism—"the god that failed." Campaigns to root out religion in the USSR, China, and Cambodia did not succeed. If anything, they proved that human beings are innately religious animals who demand a spiritual horizon that extends beyond patriotism and the promise of economic happiness. Anyone who bets that religion will vanish in the near future should be prepared to lose the wager.

Currently, we are experiencing widespread disillusionment with organized religion, an explosion of interest in spirituality and new forms of ritual, and a resurgent interest in fundamentalism. Unmoved by your inherited Judaism? Give Zen Buddhism a try. If that is too organized and ritualistic, you might find Transcendental Meditation to your liking. Tired of the missionary position? For flexible spirits there are many varieties of yoga ranging from sweating Bikram to erotic Tantra that offer the added benefit of keeping you trim and flexible. For the more vigorous there are the ancient and modern martial arts—judo, tai chi, karate, and aikido—any of which will train you in the art of following the Tao and going with the flow. There is African drumming and chanting. There are retreat centers, ashrams, and spas where you can sit at the feet of gurus, philosophers, wise men and women, and study the spiritual teachings of any tradition that may interest you. You can borrow a leaf from Native American religion and purify yourself at a sweat lodge, undertake a vision quest, or sample peyote or other psychedelics guaranteed to change your perspective on the world.

But something crucial is missing in this smorgasbord. Overall, the movement toward spirituality suffers from excessive individualism and does little to address our endemic problem of isolation, alienation, and loneliness. Additionally, the notion of individual spirituality is an existential oxymoron. In the process that leads toward spiritual maturity, we move from the singular to the plural, from I to we. In the beginning, the exploration of elemental emotions connected with the awareness of the sacred may be a matter of individual experience, but their celebration and enactment in rite and ritual requires a community.

Americans, especially, live in a lonely crowd and repress the instinctual need to belong, to be known, to be part of a welcoming community. We are herd animals. Deprived of community, we fall into a kind of cultural manic depression, alternating frantic activity and consumerism with bouts of depression. But the void remains. Caring communities are a powerful antidote to the pathological individualism and loneliness that haunts so many modern men and women.

For better and worse, religion has traditionally provided us with a necessary condition for living a fully human life—community. Now more than ever, progressive religious communities need to promote dialogue. In recent years we have been exposed to a wide range of resources from all the world religions that offer us a richer spiritual life than that of the old parochial religious communities. With the wealth of practices now available—chanting, meditation, dance, martial arts, contemplative prayer, trance, silence, healing, drumming, vision quests, and pilgrimages, to name just a few—there is no reason to remain only a Christian, only a Muslim, or only a Jew. Ours is an age that invites us to hold our traditions and institutions lightly, and to become explorers of the wide repertoire of spiritual practices.

Why do we need rituals and sacraments?

Because we fall into forgetfulness. The Speed Demon captures our souls. We are too busy. As Wordsworth wrote: "Getting and spending, we lay waste our powers; little we see in Nature that is ours." The demands of modern life are so many that we easily become distracted and neglect to pause and consider what is really important.

Rituals and sacrament are mnemonic devices that remind us to pay attention to our fragile, fleeting days, to be grateful for the gift of life, to be compassionate to other beings.

We also need communities—churches, mosques, synagogues, and temples—to preside over public rites and ceremonies that sanctify our transitions from one stage of life to another. Think of all the passages you have experienced in your journey (thus far). Have these passages been ritualized and celebrated—or not?

Birth. What rituals attended your birth?

Baptism. Confirmation. Circumcision. What beliefs came along with your membership in your parents' community?

Name giving. Who named you? Why? What name would you have chosen? Did you change your name when you married? Why? Have you gone through such radical changes in your life that you would like to choose a new name? How would you create a renaming ceremony?

Coming of age. Did you have any formal ceremonies connected with your transition from childhood to adulthood? Were you initiated into the mysteries of manhood or womanhood by any elders?

Marriage. How was your marriage celebrated? Were you married in a civil or a religious ceremony? Do you observe anniversaries? How?

Childbearing. Was childbearing a biological function experienced by your mother or a sacred event in which both parents participated? How was it celebrated? By your extended family? By intimate friends? By the community?

Growing old. When did you become old? Why? Did you have any ceremony in which you celebrated moving into this new stage of life?

Sickening and healing. How do you understand illness? As a purely biological condition? As a lack of harmony between body, mind, and spirit? Who has presided over your healing? Physicians? Psychotherapists? Ministers? Spiritual healers? What ceremonies were involved?

Dying. Where would you like to die? Who would you like to attend you at the time of your death? What rituals and sacraments would you like to have performed? Extreme unction? A final party with family and friends?

Burial. Design your funeral. How should your life be remembered and celebrated? By whom?

In each of these great transitions we stand at a boundary between the known and the unknown. Because we have never been this way before, we often depend on religious institutions that offer us time-honored protocols. This is well and good, but we may choose to improvise our own rites of passage.

Think of the common elements familiar to us all—earth, air, fire, and water—as a kit for creating rites of passage and sacraments.

Bread, wine: to express gratitude for the bounty of the land

Water: for purification, baptizing the young, preparing the dead for burial

Seeds: to teach us about birth, death, and resurrection

Music: to re-enchant the seasons and rhythms of our lives

Peyote, mescaline, and fasting: to open the doors of perception so we may taste the excess that leads to wisdom

Dancing: so we may be moved by enthusiasm, escape the prison of daily consciousness, be possessed by the Divine Spirit

Pilgrimage: journey to the faraway, to the luminous darkness of great cathedrals redolent with the piety of ages past, to high mountains where the wind inspires awe, to the sculpted red rock of canyon lands where the howl of coyotes may echo endlessly in the night

> These simple elements,
> assorted beads.
> String them as you will:
> to make a rosary,
> to remind yourself,
> to pay attention,

to practice gratitude,

to love without reason,

to garner community,

to make a sacrament of your life.

• • •

Now that my family is far-flung, I no longer have a Special Day Candle to mark pivotal events. But each morning I brew the tea, toast the bread, and bring the elements of communion to the bed where my wife and I usher in the day with a prayer of gratitude.

7

Communities of Concern and the Quest for Justice

What does the Lord require of you but to do justice, to love mercy and to walk humbly with your God?

—Micah 6:8

Sacred vision culminates in the struggle to *do* the truth. Justice is where the rubber meets the road, where spiritual practice passes from the realm of feeling to the realm of action, where the heroic journey turns away from private spirituality to the chaotic world of politics. The essence of a sacred life is not passionate belief in any of the aliases of God but a disposition to feel compassion for others and to act on that feeling.

Our journey now leads in a direction many who have been on a spiritual quest but wanted nothing to do with religion will find puzzling, for the way forward leads not away from but directly into the heart of religion. For those who have suffered the poisonous practices of so much institutional religion, it is astonishing to discover that the insight that gave birth to religion should now offer us the antidote. The root meaning of *religion* comes from the Latin *ligare,* which means "to bind, connect, or reconnect." In this original sense, *religion* bears nearly the opposite meaning it has been assigned in modern culture. In essence, religion is not about cult, creed, or ceremonies (bell, book, and candle). It is not about miracle, mystery, and authority. It is not about a transcendent God made known to us by prophets, scriptures, priests, and institutions. It is not even about faith. It is about recognizing and cherishing the sacred bonds that hold all living beings together in a single community.

In the beginning is We. The crucial insight that was born out of the religious impulse is the awareness that we are bound to the cosmos and the political commonwealth in which we dwell. The self is never alone but is always undergirded by a network of relationships that bind and nurture, limit and enhance. Community is not the result of a social contract between autonomous individuals but the substance from which we emerge. Humans are cosmopolitan beings, informed by and belonging to the cosmos and the polis, a body of citizens. Therefore, authentic religion and spirituality cannot be separated from politics—only sectarian, nationalistic, and idolatrous politics.

This vision of the human condition implicit in the original meaning of religion offers a necessary corrective to our contemporary emphasis on spirituality. If religion has been unfairly vilified by modern atheologians, spirituality has been uncritically embraced. Because the notion of spirituality is vague and all too often promises tranquility, prosperity, and enlightenment without any real sacrifice, it arouses little opposition or critique. The new spirituality has been at pains to distinguish itself from Sunday-go-to-meeting religion and denominational worship. It is enthusiastic, warm, and experimental in its pursuit of a new experience of the sacred. But, alas, it has been largely irrelevant to the great social, political, and economic problems we face. It doesn't do soup kitchens, civil rights protests, or demonstrations against the Pentagon.

For three decades I have lectured and offered seminars at institutes and retreat centers frequented by modern pilgrims in search of spirituality. For the most part I have applauded their investigations into the depths of the psyche and their experimentation with non-Western forms of spiritual practice. But recently I have grown increasingly dissatisfied. What compels my attention is the simple observation that amid all the offerings on holistic living, healing, meditation, awareness, opening the heart, oneness, knowing God, and sacred bodywork, there is little or no reference to justice. Unsurprisingly, the new spirituality has produced no liberation movement, no Bonhoeffer, Niebuhr, Gandhi, Dorothy Day, Martin Luther King Jr., Cesar Chavez, or William Sloane Coffin who speaks, prays, organizes, and puts moral pressure on the privileged and the powerful.

To be concerned with spirituality but ignore the struggle for justice is as much of an oxymoron as compassionate egotism. The vision that all creatures belong within a single community leads, necessarily, to a commitment to practice justice, to seek the harmony of the whole, to recognize the priority of law over the self-interest of any individual, race, religion, or class. For better and worse we are members of one another—a community of justice-in-the-making.

From the time of Amos and the Hebrew prophets, of Socrates and the Greek philosophers, our experiments with democratic government have been based on the idea of justice. The great epic that sets Western culture apart is as much the story of an evolving communal quest for greater justice as it is the story of the individual's heroic quest. Generation after generation the body politic has steadily, if reluctantly and stumblingly, yielded to the pressure from the dispossessed and edged toward greater justice for all. Gradually, the nonpersons who have been denied political rights since the time of the Greeks—slaves; women; children; religious, ethnic, and sexual minorities—have been enfranchised.

This ancient, evolving but unfulfilled vision of justice for all offers an organizing paradigm and vocation for the twenty-first century, a place where religion and politics can productively join hands. Lacking a universally accepted revealed religion or a world government to unite humankind, we might find what we have looked for in the sky under our feet, in the humus that is foundation of all human community—the quest for justice. A heroic effort to enact ecological justice, political justice, and economic justice is the only communal crusade that could result in a relatively peaceful world by the end of this century.

ENACTING JUSTICE

The moment we begin to think about how justice is to be enacted we are plunged into a tangled web of issues about the relationship between politics and religion. We'd best begin by distinguishing different responsibilities that fall to various communities.

The primary responsibility for enacting justice belongs to the nation or state. The social contract that is the basis of all civility demands that every citizen receive his due measure of justice. In practice, ruling elites usually define what is due to different segments of the population in a very prejudicial manner. Even America, which preaches liberty and justice for all, continues to practice inequality for minorities, women, and the poor. In contemporary Islamic society, a woman has one-half the legal status of a man. However, notwithstanding the perennial failures of governments to provide justice for their citizens, this remains their primary responsibility.

Communities of the concerned—both religious institutions and the numerous "secular" NGOs such as Amnesty International, Sierra Club, Greenpeace, Doctors Without Borders, and Save the Children that are animated by a vision of the sacredness of all life—have unique responsibilities.

1. They demand that all living beings be treated with respect and reverence. Their impulse to struggle for justice rests on recognition of the sacred and the awareness that injustice is a form of sacrilege.

2. They take the initiative in spelling out the principles of justice. Exactly what is the minimum owed to any citizen?

3. They protest and organize against the persons and agencies responsible for injustice and demand that governments fulfill their mandate to render justice to all citizens. History shows us that sovereign states and nations continually fail at this task. Power trumps justice. Special interests trample the common good.

Greed displaces fairness. Indifference destroys compassion. To bring these transgressions to an end, communities of the concerned keep pressure on governments. Thou shall not torture prisoners, oppress the poor, commit genocide, use weapons of mass destruction, lay waste the land, destroy the nest of the meadowlark or the lair of the lion, pollute living streams or the ceaseless sea, foul the free-roaming wind, prostitute the bodies of women, children, and men, or treasure wealth above compassion. When these moral standards are violated, they become the outraged conscience of the body politic, the voice of the cosmopolitan citizen.

4. Communities animated by a sense of reverence go beyond the requirement of justice to consider what love demands of us. The law does not require that we love our neighbors, only that we render them their due. These communities hold themselves to a higher standard and strive to find ways to provide charity and care for the dispossessed, the powerless, and the poor.

PRINCIPLES OF JUSTICE

The first challenge facing communities of the concerned is to articulate the principles governing ecological, political, and economic justice and give us a vision of an ideal toward which we may aspire. What private lifestyles and public policies are required by the belief that all beings deserve to be treated with respect? What are the sacred obligations we must honor if we are to survive and thrive in a globalized world?

Where should we begin to think about justice? With the political order? The economic order? The ecological order?

In large measure, our contemporary crisis is the result of a modern ideology that places economic rights first, political rights second, and ecological rights a distant third. The wealthy, "democratic" countries have been willing to tolerate third world dictators who abuse the civil rights of their citizens and create ecological disasters so long as they keep the world safe for business. This suggests that we must reverse our priorities. Our first consideration must be ecological justice because environmental integrity is absolutely necessary for the survival of the human community. If we destroy our environment, justice for the disinherited and poor becomes a moot point.

ECOLOGICAL JUSTICE

Of all forms of justice, ecological justice is the easiest to conceptualize and the most difficult to imagine achieving in a world suffering from both overpopulation and an economic system based on the self-interest of multinational corporations. Our quest for justice needs to begin with the nonhuman members of our commonwealth because they are absolutely powerless, while the human poor are only relatively powerless. Those suffering most from ecological injustice—the myriad nonhuman species and the yet unborn—lack sufficient advocates and political power to protect their rights.

The principles that provide the foundation for the practice of *ecological* justice are:

1. Each living person has the right to a share of the natural endowment of the land, water, and air that is necessary to sustain life. You shall not steal this from your neighbors.

2. Persons yet unborn have the same right to an equal share of the natural endowment as those now living. You shall not steal from future generations by squandering limited resources.

3. Nonhuman beings also have a right to an environment necessary to sustain life. You shall not steal this from any other sentient inhabitants of the commonwealth. (What does this tell us about hunting, preservation of wilderness, the extinction of species?)

4. No persons, nations, or species have the right to exceed the carrying capacity of the earth. Clearly, we must learn to live within the limits of our resources, or the entire community of living beings will suffer. You shall not steal from the future. (An old Gary Larson cartoon showing two deer in a forest gets at the heart of the matter. One deer says to the other, "Why can't they thin their own goddamn herds?" *The ecological problem is the population problem.*)

Item: Scientists estimate that the carrying capacity of the earth would allow our present population an ecological footprint of 1.7 hectares per person with 0.3 set aside for nonhuman species. At present, the average ecological footprint is 2.8 hectares, which is 40 percent larger than the available space necessary for producing food, fuel, and forestry products on a sustainable basis. The per capita ecological footprint in the United States is 10.3 hectares.

POLITICAL JUSTICE

At this stage in world history, the United States Bill of Rights probably gives us the most realistic list of the rights necessary for living in a political community and provides a minimal standard against which to measure the progress or regress of nations. (The United Nations Universal Declaration of Human Rights is more a wish list than a realistic political standard, proposing as it does that everyone has the right to a job and a paid vacation.)

The principles that provide the foundation for the practice of global political justice look like this:

1. To be a member of a community is to be entitled to an equal share in the commons—rights, privileges, responsibilities, and resources.

2. In a global world order, what affects one country affects all countries; therefore, a bill of rights for all citizens is a hygienic requirement for a healthy commonwealth. You can't have massive abuse of civil rights in Zimbabwe, Darfur, or Tibet without having an effect on South Africa, the United States, or Germany.

3. Civil rights cannot be maintained without institutions to enforce them. An emerging global community requires nations to surrender a larger measure of their sovereignty to institutions of transnational governance. It demands the creation of effective peacekeeping forces and the recognition of the authority of the International Criminal Court to punish those guilty of crimes against any member of the global commonwealth.

4. In a global commonwealth, the rule of universal jurisdiction must apply. All nations are responsible for prosecuting genocide and crimes against humanity no matter where they are committed, and for punishing the guilty.

Item: In 2002 the International Criminal Court, a body invested with the authority to deal with cases of genocide and crimes against humanity, moved from dream to reality as it was ratified by more than eighty nations. Unfortunately for the cause of global justice, the United States is bucking the trend and undercutting the efforts of other countries to strengthen the international rule of law by its refusal to submit itself to the World Court at The Hague or the International Criminal Court, by violating the Comprehensive Nuclear-Test-Ban Treaty, and by ignoring the Kyoto Protocol on climate change.

ECONOMIC JUSTICE

Because economics dominated the values and worldview of the twentieth century it must be considered last in the twenty-first century. Traditional theories of dealing with the fair distribution of wealth have applied only within the limits of national borders. But we live in an increasingly globalized world that lacks any theory for dealing with the catastrophic gap in wealth between the minority of rich nations and the majority of poor.

How *should* the goods and services created by a global economy be distributed? Do the wealthy owe anything to the two billion men, women, and children who live on less than two dollars per day? What is implicitly owed to any individual who is forced by the need to survive to abandon village life to work in cities such as Calcutta or São Paulo?

Extrapolating from the democratic principle "No taxation without representation" leads to "No globalization without representation." Anyone who is forced into the global economic system has the right to participate in its decisions. And in the kingdom of economics, representation means having money to spend.

The principle that a universal right to a reasonable amount of money is conferred on all citizens of the global economic system leads to questions that make the average CEO squirm. What do global corporations owe to global citizens? What percentage of the profits of any private corporation is owed to the public? What is a fair level of profit for a corporation? What is an unjust level? At what point should there be a cap on profits distributed to executives and stockholders and the surplus given to the least advantaged members of the global economic community?

The principles that provide the foundation for the practice of global economic justice are:

1. We live in a single global community that depends on the joint action of suppliers of raw material, producers, and consumers. This web of social interdependence entails mutual obligation and duty.

2. The community owns the economy, not vice versa. As the word suggests, we all are entitled to a share of the common-wealth.

3. The need for economic justice is based on the insight that the poverty of the parts cannot produce wealth for the whole. Abraham Lincoln warned that "a nation cannot long remain half slave and half free." Likewise, a world divided between the rich and poor cannot long avoid global civil war. The wretched of the earth will not remain pacific indefinitely. Last guys don't finish nice.

4. Justice demands that the poorest consumer is due a share of the wealth that is necessary to survive and has the right to participate in the process that creates wealth. All persons are not created equal in talent, ambition, or access to education and economic opportunity. Thus a reasonable degree of economic inequality is not necessarily a sign of injustice. But when the

world's 225 richest people now have a combined wealth of $1 trillion (which is equal to the combined annual income of the world's 2.5 billion poorest people), only someone completely lacking in moral sensitivity, empathy, and compassion can ignore the glaring injustice.

Something must be done. But what? And by whom? The very notion of economic justice has come to seem like an oxymoron. As some wag said, modern economics operates on the basis of a new golden rule: Those who have the gold make the rules. The corporate law of maximum profit for the stockholders is in conflict with the prophetic law of justice for all, which derives from the deeper principle of reverence for life.

To secure greater justice for all we need to refocus economics away from our obsession with gross national product and toward the ideal of gross national happiness (Bhutan's byword). Economic policy should promote small-scale local solutions that pay special attention to the rights of women and rural communities. Micro-loan programs, such as those begun by the Grameen Bank in Bangladesh, have created a generation of small entrepreneurs and have advanced gender equality. To keep the rural poor from flocking to the even poorer cities, most third world countries need to abandon their current emphasis on export-driven agriculture and promote sustainable agricultural development in order to feed local populations. Greater justice demands the protection of local industry and the integrity of village life based on community control of the inflow and outflow of capital.

We need to reconceptualize and reorganize our economic institutions to create conditions for the well-being of all global citizens. The old economy of scarcity, competition, and accumulation of wealth by the elite could, at best, afford to guarantee minimal rights to the masses. A new economy might be prosperous enough to guarantee all persons that expanded list of rights envisioned by the framers of the UN Universal Declaration of Human Rights.

Item: The UN Development Program reports that as of 2006 the richest 20 percent of nations make 86 percent of consumer purchases, consume 58 percent of energy, account for 53 percent of carbon dioxide emissions, use two-thirds of the earth's carrying capacity, account for 82 percent of expanding export trade and 68 percent of direct investment. The poorest 20 percent make .3 percent of consumer purchases, consume 4 percent of energy, account for 3 percent of carbon dioxide emissions, and account for 1 percent of expanding trade and direct investment. Some 1.2 billion people survive on $1 per day or less and lack access to safe drinking water; 3 billion exist on less than $2 per day. The UN Development Program estimates that $9 billion would provide water and sanitation for all, $12 billion would cover reproductive health for all women, $13 billion would give every person on earth basic health and nutrition, and $6 billion would provide basic education.

AGENTS OF JUSTICE

Insofar as governments so frequently fail in their responsibility, by whom is justice to be enacted?

There is an ancient legend found in both Judaism and Islam that God is frequently tempted to destroy the world because of its weight of wickedness and injustice. But generation after generation it is spared by the presence of thirty-six just men who quietly commit acts of kindness and compassion. Not only are the thirty-six anonymous, they are, in all likelihood, unknown even to themselves.

In our generation there has been a blossoming of agents of Justice—36 × 36 × 36 × 36. Millions of communities of concern have sprung up all over the world. NGOs have joined with traditional religious institutions to care for the dispossessed and downtrodden poor. And untold millions of private citizens and philanthropic foundations acting alone or in concert with others have become entrepreneurs of justice, dedicated to the welfare of others.

Savor this random list of caring organizations and recall what you already know of their missions, and you get a good idea of the myriad ways in which the quest for justice is being pursued in self-generated communities of concern.

Church World Service
Human Rights Watch
Amnesty International
Friends World Committee
Doctors Without Borders
Save the Children
Heifer International
Oxfam
UNESCO
World Vision
Red Cross
Africa Action
Amazon Watch
CARE
Cousteau Society / Equipe Cousteau
Democracy Watch
Freedom House

Global Vision
Peace Corps
Greenpeace
Physicians for Social Responsibility

What this list reveals is that the now and future agents of justice are driven by a mix of secular, religious, and spiritual motives. The old distinctions between religious and secular are being subsumed within these new communities whose members are dedicated to some common action. We are seeing Christian fundamentalists making common cause with environmentalists to fight ecological blight and faith-based churches joining with NGOs and government agencies to fight the AIDS epidemic and bring food to millions of displaced persons. Philanthropic foundations are monitoring elections in countries recently emerging from tyrannical and corrupt government.

The emergence of these new communities of concern is hope made manifest in charitable action. Just men and women are putting the civil back in civilization and keeping alive the dialogue between love, power, and justice.

VIOLENCE
Sacred Vision and Tragic Action

Let me say, at the risk of seeming ridiculous, that the true
revolutionary is guided by great feelings of love.

—CHE GUEVARA

Before leaving the quest for justice, we need to wrestle
with a difficult moral conundrum—the troubling question of the use of violence in the service of justice. Perhaps the greatest failure of organized religion has been its
tendency to sanctify violence by the state. By embracing
an ideology of God and country, holy war, jihad, and crusade, the enemy of the moment is cast in the role of
enemy of God, infidel, or member of an axis of evil. Thus
dehumanized, he ceases to be a sacred being and may be
killed without guilt or remorse.

The issue of violence and the sacred is complex and
involves great moral ambiguity.

When we consider genocide in Bosnia, Rwanda, and
Darfur it is hard to escape the conclusion that greater justice would have been done had the United Nations' Peacekeeping force used violent means to stop the slaughter.

And if we remember the systemic violence and denial of civil rights by repressive regimes—Hitler's Germany, Stalin's Soviet Union, South Africa's apartheid government, et cetera—it is easy to make the case that, under such repressive conditions, an effective effort to enact justice involves the willingness to use deadly force. As Marx noted, the powerful and privileged never give up their position voluntarily.

The great temptation is to baptize the strategic violence necessary to destroy those who perpetrate the systemic violence of entrenched regimes. But it is precisely in such situations that caring communities need to insist that violence, even when necessary, is not sacred. All living beings, including our enemies of the moment, deserve to be treated in a respectful manner. The commandment "Love your enemies" does not propose passive acceptance of intolerable injustice or forswearing all use of violence. What it forbids is systematic dehumanization of the enemy that makes killing a morally neutral act. When unavoidable, the use of violence in the service of justice is a tragic necessity. There may be just wars. There are never sacred wars. It is the burden of communities with some vision of the sacred to keep us aware of the tragic dimension of warfare. Killing, even in self-defense or to prevent the slaughter of the innocent, still involves a primal blood guilt that we have conspired to deny in modern times.

The enemy we kill, no matter his evil deeds, remains a many-splendored human being with failings. It is only by remembering the sacredness of all living beings that we limit tragic violence.

I suspect that the inordinate number of cases of post-traumatic stress syndrome we are seeing in soldiers returning from combat is in large measure due to an unacknowledged condition of moral dissonance. The modern military indoctrinates its members in the profane ideology that killing is a duty, which does not involve guilt. It does not prepare soldiers for the experience of the tragic moral burden that stems from killing. Returning from the battlefield, our modern warriors are offered no rituals to assuage the guilt they feel.

By keeping alive both the vision of the sacred and the awareness of the moral ambiguity involved in violent action, sacramental communities point beyond guilt to the possibility of healing. In place of the artificial innocence that profane cultures offer their wounded warriors, churches and other sacred communities provide powerful rituals of confession and repentance that allow their members to experience forgiveness and to be renewed.

●   ●   ●

Ex nihilo. From the fertile void, the aching emptiness where *ought* is more real than *is,* comes a silent testimony to an ideal order that makes its demands on us regardless of our ability to conform.

Not that old Freudian conscience, the superego, the watching institution, the internalized eyes of parents, peers, and patriarchs that pin us in the spotlight and accuse us of transgressions too numerous and vague to index. Not the paranoid conscience of the tribal psyche, the trumpet of patriotism summoning us to arms to defend Us against Them, the inhumanly evil enemy against whom we must wage holy war in the name of God and Country.

It is uncompromising. It flies no flag. It issues from somewhere beyond common laws of good and evil and requires what is impractical by any pragmatic standard. Call it "the transmoral conscience" (Tillich) or the ontological conscience. It is an echo sounding forth in our depths urging us to become essentially human. The sound of pure spirit breaking against the shore of time.

EPILOGUE

The Re-enchantment
of Everyday Life

Spirit:
The invisible beacon
that lights the way
along forgotten paths
to a remembered homeland.

—SANDOR MCNAB

We have been a long time coming, after painful leave-taking from homes and lands in which we were comfortable, through deserts and oases where we discovered that our soul could only thrive in a sacred place. In the end we return to the disenchanted communities from which we originally took flight because there is no place else to go. For better and worse, this is our one and only earth. It remains for us to discover how we may, at once, be at rest and in transit, ordinary people on an unending heroic journey, living in a fractured and enchanted world.

•   •   •

The fate of our times is characterized by rationalization
and intellectualization and, above all, by the disenchantment of the world.

—Max Weber

If there is any secret to this life I live, this is it: The sound
of what cannot be seen sings within everything that can.

—<noreply@storypeople.com>

A long time ago, before there were malls, CAT scans, and
electronic networks linking us in a disembodied global village, humankind dwelled in a wondrous community of
myriad beings within a welcoming cosmos. Every niche in
the great chain of being that stretched from the highest
heavens to the unfathomed depths of the seas was thought
to be inhabited by some helping spirit—god, goddess,
angel, fairy, sylph, elf—or by some sinister ghost, monster,
devil, or demon that went bump in the night. In this
animistic universe, trees, streams, and mountains were
thought to be alive and have personalities, to have a voice
no less than humans, birds, or bears. The world was enchanted.

Laurens van der Post grew up in Africa among the

Bushmen and describes their world in his marvelous book *Patterns of Renewal.* "The Bushman, the first man, lived in an extraordinary intimacy with nature. There was nowhere that he did not feel he belonged. . . . He had none of that dreadful sense of not belonging, of isolation, of meaninglessness that so devastates the heart of modern man. Wherever he went he belonged. We are a generation of know-alls but few of us have the life-giving feeling of being known. . . . Wherever this little man went he was known. The trees knew him; the animals knew him as he knew them; the stars knew him. His sense of relationship was so vivid that he could speak of 'our brother the Vulture.'"

The history of disenchantment is well enough known to need no repeating. Ironically, the process of secularization and disenchantment—"killing of the great god Pan," as D. H. Lawrence called it—was the result of the unlikely collusion of religion and science. The three great monotheistic religions that came to dominate Western culture gradually suppressed animism, desanctified nature, and focused reverence on a transcendent God. The world may have been created by God, but it was to be used, not worshipped. Once the spirits were banished from nature, the profane environment could be probed by scientific intelligence and altered endlessly by technological ingenuity. The disenchantment of nature and the triumph of scientific method were the means by which humankind gained the confidence and power to become the architect of its own destiny.

But much was lost when we swapped enchantment for power. As the materialistic paradigm of modern science shaped our experience, the world increasingly became an arena of problems to be solved rather than a sacred habitat created for the fulfillment of some divine purpose. The disenchanted world provided us with a cornucopia of goods and blessings, but it became a lonely place, devoid of gods.

Some have suggested that new holistic science re-enchants the cosmos. Philosopher and scientist Ervin Laszlo argues that contemporary quantum physicists, astronomers, cosmologists, and biophysicists are converging on a new vision of the cosmos as an entangled system evolving toward coherence and wholeness through interconnection and interaction—more like a living organism than a machine. Such new science breaks us out of the prison of the old deterministic, mechanistic universe ruled by the strict law of cause and effect.

> At the cutting edge of contemporary science a remarkable insight is surfacing: the universe, with all things in it, is a quasi-living, coherent whole. All things in it are connected. . . . A cosmos that is connected, coherent and whole recalls an ancient notion that was present in the

tradition of every civilization: it is an enchanted
cosmos. . . . We are part of each other and of nature.
We are a conscious part of the world, a being through
which the cosmos comes to know itself. . . . We are at
home in the universe.

—ERVIN LASZLO

This holistic scientific vision gives us reasons to believe that we are integral parts of a meaningful whole. Its language of emergent self-organizing systems, quantum vacuums, plenum voids, and a metaverse that gives rise to recurring cycles of universes, inspires our imaginations to soar free. It strongly suggests that this cosmos in which we find ourselves is no collection of inert particles, full of sound and fury signifying nothing. It is more like a "thou" than an "it." We are meant to be here.

But reason and theory alone can never lead us out of our exile back to our enchanted homeland. To fill the G-d-shaped vacuum and regain the feeling of belonging we must recover the wisdom of the heart. I am not certain how to reestablish an intimate connection with the world we inhabit, but one rule of thumb I follow when my philosophical quest comes to a roadblock is to turn around to see where I came from.

When I study the etymology of a word, for instance,

I often uncover the metaphor that points back to the experience that gave birth to the word. *Enchant* comes via the French *enchanter,* meaning "to bewitch, charm," which in turn derived from the Latin *incantare,* which was used to describe the effect of magic spells but literally meant "to sing." This suggests that enchantment is not something we do but something that is done to us. In the presence of the sacred we are entranced. We are addressed by melody, by the chorus of our neighbors within our commonwealth—birds, insects, animals—and by the distant music of the spheres.

Bernie Krause has wandered the world recording all kinds of soundscapes and creature choruses: elk, wolves, jaguars, whales, ants, crabs, and crickets. We are surrounded by natural symphonies. Arise early and listen to the dawn chorus, and you will find yourself swept up—enchanted—by a spontaneous musical performance by a multitude of diverse voices.

> Considered listening . . . is quiet and gentle. It is designed to create a new understanding, a gathering of kindred spirits, human and otherwise, which can lead to discoveries about how we all make our presence known . . . the creature world has stories to divulge that are nothing short of amazing.
>
> —BERNIE KRAUSE

The world is alive with the sound of music. It is we who are deaf. Disenchantment is an inevitable consequence of our failure to listen. How could we possibly be enchanted by the voices of our wild neighbors when we are too distracted, too inundated by our own din to listen? Even if we do pause to listen to a mockingbird, we assume its songs are mindless sounds.

In a sacred soundscape, listening comes before understanding, silence before speech. Scientific experts assure me that frogs sing only to one another. I know better. Their chorus informs me that my amphibian kin who share this habitat are flourishing. They request that I take care of the fields where they grab a tasty grasshopper and the swampy area along the creek where they gather for choir practice every evening.

Re-enchantment begins when we listen to the wild music and biophanies that surround us, and to the appeals made to us by others. Stripped of its animistic mythology, the core of enchantment is being addressed by the voices of beings to whom we are joined by community and obligation. Whether the voice of the other is a homeless person asking for help or a wood thrush shattering the crystal dawn with one pure note, it addresses me with a gift and a demand. Beneath the myriad voices there is a single song, "I am, I am, I am," that calls for my attention, appreciation, and reverence.

Two of the greatest theologians of our age, one Protestant, the other Jewish, remind us that we are always being addressed by the voices of other beings and by events that seem to merely happen to us.

> All things and all men, so to speak, call on us with small or loud voices. They want us to listen, they want us to understand their intrinsic claims, their justice of being. . . . But we can give it to them only through the love which listens.
>
> —PAUL TILLICH

> What occurs to me addresses me. In what occurs to me the world-happening addresses me.
>
> —MARTIN BUBER

In order to move closer to the experience of re-enchantment we need to go a step further—beyond Buber's metaphor of a dialogue between I and Thou, of being addressed by a distant God. Mircea Eliade, the great historian of religion, reports a practice that also serves as a metaphor that will lead us a step further in the journey toward re-enchantment. According to Eliade, the Australian aboriginal tribe the Achilpa, in their wanderings, carried a pole representing the cosmic axis, which they planted in the ground whenever they came to rest. This sacred pole was originally given them by the divine being Numbakula, and it provided the means to organize and sanctify all the land that radiated out from it. Possessing this portable cosmic axis gave the tribe an opening to the transcendent and a means to remain always on holy ground, at the center of the world. This symbolism of dwelling in a consecrated cosmos is widespread among native cultures. Among the Hopi it includes the idea that the human spine is also an *axis mundi,* a cosmic center.

It is this experience of living at the center of the cosmos that is necessary to re-enchant everyday life. Our existence is the immanence and the incarnation of the cosmos. We are the cosmos becoming Moses, Jesus, Muhammad, the Dalai Lama, Barack Obama, Earl Scott, Patricia de Jong, or Sam Keen for a fleeting moment. It fulfills its mysterious purposes through us, beckoning with a whispered song of hope toward a future we cannot imagine.

We fragile creatures, atoms in an infinite ocean of beings, are formed by indescribably complex processes over eons of evolution. Yet each of us resides at the center of the cosmos. All the energies, currents, and intelligent powers that have ever been flow through the vibratory centers (chakras) of our minds and bodies. It takes an entire universe to create an Einstein or a spotted owl. We are each cosmocentric.

This holy land, this enchanted commonwealth of sacred beings without number, is where we belong. It is the place for which we have always longed.

Welcome home.

ACKNOWLEDGMENTS

A book is less the work of a solitary author than it is an interplay of voices—a symposium, sometimes sedate, sometimes drunken. My thoughts and ideas have emerged from dialogues with a host of philosophers, psychologists, theologians, poets, artists, and daily companions, some living, some officially dead but spiritually immortal. Without their presence my mind would be monolithic and poverty-stricken. In addition, I struggle with a squad of worthy opponents—true believers and atheists, fundamentalists of all stripes, who approach religion without a sense of humor or a love of poetry. *In the Absence of God* is dedicated to all who appear in its pages. It belongs as much to them as to me. And to my friend and agent, Ned Leavitt, who does battle for me against the legions of Mammon; to my editor, Peter Guzzardi, who cut, slashed, and shed much red ink in the service of clarity; to my allies at Harmony Books—Shaye Areheart, Julia Pastore, and the many others who escorted this book through the wilderness.

INDEX

ABOUT THE AUTHOR

SAM KEEN is a noted author and lecturer who has written a baker's dozen books on philosophy, religion, propaganda, birds, and the flying trapeze. He holds graduate degrees from Harvard and a Ph.D. from Princeton. He was for many years a professor at various legitimate colleges and universities before going on a sabbatical from which he never returned, preferring to become an editor of *Psychology Today* and a freelance writer and workshop leader. He coproduced the Emmy-nominated PBS documentary *Faces of the Enemy* and was the subject of a PBS special with Bill Moyers titled *Your Mythic Journey*. When not traveling around the world lecturing and doing seminars on a wide range of topics, Keen cuts wood, tends his farm in the hills above Sonoma, California, takes long hikes, and practices the flying trapeze (awkwardly but with enthusiasm).

Visit him at www.samkeen.com